Criminal Justice, Law Enforcement and Corrections Series

DIGITAL SURVEILLANCE: LAWS, SECURITY AND RELATED ISSUES

CRIMINAL JUSTICE, LAW ENFORCEMENT AND CORRECTIONS

Homicide Investigations
Allan B. Smythe (Editor)
2009 ISBN 978-1-60692-258-3

Mass Incarceration and Offender Registry in the United States
Russell D. Javitze (Editor)
2009 ISBN 978-1-60692-657-4

Batterer Intervention: Program Approaches and Criminal Justice Strategies
Kerry Healey, Christine Smith and Chris O'Sullivan
2009 ISBN 978-1-60692-934-6

Digital Surveillance: Laws, Security and Related Issues
Joseph G. Massingale (Editor)
2009 ISBN 978-1-60692-312-2

Criminal Justice, Law Enforcement and Corrections Series

DIGITAL SURVEILLANCE: LAWS, SECURITY AND RELATED ISSUES

JOSEPH G. MASSINGALE
EDITOR

Nova Science Publishers, Inc.
New York

For permission to use material from this book please contact us:
Telephone 631-231-7269; Fax 631-231-8175
Web Site: http://www.novapublishers.com

LIBRARY OF CONGRESS CATALOGING-IN-PUBLICATION DATA

Available upon request.
ISBN: 978-1-60692-312-2

Published by Nova Science Publishers, Inc. ✝ New York

CONTENTS

PREFACE

New digital technologies and wireless services have altered the character of electronic surveillance. This book deals with some of the laws and technologies that are are being utilized to cope with the rapid advances in digital technologies as it relates to crime and homeland security.

Chapter 1 - The Communications Assistance for Law Enforcement Act (CALEA, P.L. 103- 414, 47 U.S.C. 1001-1010), enacted October 25, 1994, is intended to preserve the ability of law enforcement officials to conduct electronic surveillance effectively and efficiently despite the deployment of new digital technologies and wireless services that have altered the character of electronic surveillance. CALEA requires telecommunications carriers to modify their equipment, facilities, and services, wherever reasonably achievable, to ensure that they are able to comply with authorized electronic surveillance actions.

Since 2004, the Federal Communications Commission (FCC) has been considering a number of questions as to how to apply CALEA to new technologies, such as Voice over Internet Protocol (VoIP). In August 2005, in response to a March 2004 petition by a group of law enforcement agencies, the FCC released a Notice of Proposed Rulemaking and Declaratory Ruling which required providers of certain broadband and interconnected VoIP services to accommodate law enforcement wiretaps. The FCC found that these services could be considered replacements for conventional telecommunications services already subject to wiretap rules, including circuit-switched voice service and dial-up Internet access. The Order is limited to facilities-based broadband Internet access service providers and VoIP providers that offer services that use the public switched telephone network ("interconnected VoIP providers).

In May 2006, the FCC addressed several outstanding issues regarding CALEA implementation. Among other clarifications, the FCC (1) affirmed its May 14, 2007 compliance deadline for facilities-based broadband Internet access and interconnected VoIP services, and clarified that the date applied to all such providers; (2) explained that the FCC does not plan to intervene in the standards-setting process in this matter; (3) permitted telecommunications carriers the option of using Trusted Third Parties to assist in meeting their CALEA obligations; (4) restricted the availability of compliance extensions to equipment, facilities, and services deployed prior to October 25, 1998; (5) found that the FCC may enforce action under section 229(a) of the Communications Act against carriers that fail to comply with CALEA; and (6) concluded that carriers are responsible for CALEA development and implementation costs for post-January 1, 1995, equipment and facilities, and declined to adopt a national surcharge to recover CALEA costs.

In June 2006, the United States Court of Appeals for the District of Columbia Circuit affirmed the FCC's decision concluding that VoIP and facilities-based broadband Internet access providers have CALEA obligations similar to those of telephone companies.

Chapter 2 - Data mining has become one of the key features of many homeland security initiatives. Often used as a means for detecting fraud, assessing risk, and product retailing, data mining involves the use of data analysis tools to discover previously unknown, valid patterns and relationships in large data sets. In the context of homeland security, data mining can be a potential means to identify terrorist activities, such as money transfers and communications, and to identify and track individual terrorists themselves, such as through travel and immigration records.

While data mining represents a significant advance in the type of analytical tools currently available, there are limitations to its capability. One limitation is that although data mining can help reveal patterns and relationships, it does not tell the user the value or significance of these patterns. These types of determinations must be made by the user. A second limitation is that while data mining can identify connections between behaviors and/or variables, it does not necessarily identify a causal relationship. Successful data mining still requires skilled technical and analytical specialists who can structure the analysis and interpret the output.

Data mining is becoming increasingly common in both the private and public sectors. Industries such as banking, insurance, medicine, and retailing commonly use data mining to reduce costs, enhance research, and increase sales. In the public sector, data mining applications initially were used as a means to detect fraud and waste, but have grown to also be used for purposes such as measuring and improving program performance. However, some of the homeland security data mining applications represent a significant expansion in the quantity and scope of data to be analyzed. Some efforts that have attracted a higher level of congressional interest include the Terrorism Information Awareness (TIA) project (now-discontinued) and the Computer-Assisted Passenger Prescreening System II (CAPPS II) project (now- canceled and replaced by Secure Flight). Other initiatives that have been the subject of congressional interest include the Multi-State Anti-Terrorism Information Exchange (MATRIX), the Able Danger program, the Automated Targeting System (ATS), and data collection and analysis projects being conducted by the National Security Agency (NSA).

As with other aspects of data mining, while technological capabilities are important, there are other implementation and oversight issues that can influence the success of a project's outcome. One issue is data quality, which refers to the accuracy and completeness of the data being analyzed. A second issue is the interoperability of the data mining software and databases being used by different agencies. A third issue is mission creep, or the use of data for purposes other than for which the data were originally collected. A fourth issue is privacy. Questions that may be considered include the degree to which government agencies should use and mix commercial data with government data, whether data sources are being used for purposes other than those for which they were originally designed, and possible application of the Privacy Act to these initiatives. It is anticipated that congressional oversight of data mining projects will grow as data mining efforts continue to evolve.

Chapter 3 - This chapter covers the data mining activities of all elements of the ODNI. Constituent elements of the Intelligence Community are reporting their data mining activities through their own departments or agencies. This chapter covering ODNI activities is unclassified and has been made available to the public through the ODNI' s website. A classified annex has also been prepared and has been transmitted to the appropriate Congressional committees.

In: Digital Surveillance
Editor: J. G. Massingale, pp. 1-16
ISBN: 978-1-60692-312-2

Chapter 1

DIGITAL SURVEILLANCE: THE COMMUNICATIONS ASSISTANCE FOR LAW ENFORCEMENT ACT*

Patricia Moloney Figliola

ABSTRACT

The Communications Assistance for Law Enforcement Act (CALEA, P.L. 103- 414, 47 U.S.C. 1001-1010), enacted October 25, 1994, is intended to preserve the ability of law enforcement officials to conduct electronic surveillance effectively and efficiently despite the deployment of new digital technologies and wireless services that have altered the character of electronic surveillance. CALEA requires telecommunications carriers to modify their equipment, facilities, and services, wherever reasonably achievable, to ensure that they are able to comply with authorized electronic surveillance actions.

Since 2004, the Federal Communications Commission (FCC) has been considering a number of questions as to how to apply CALEA to new technologies, such as Voice over Internet Protocol (VoIP). In August 2005, in response to a March 2004 petition by a group of law enforcement agencies, the FCC released a Notice of Proposed Rulemaking and Declaratory Ruling which required providers of certain broadband and interconnected VoIP services to accommodate law enforcement wiretaps. The FCC found that these services

* This is an edited, excerpted and augmented edition of a Congressional Research Service publication, Report RL30677, dated January 29, 2008.

could be considered replacements for conventional telecommunications services already subject to wiretap rules, including circuit-switched voice service and dial-up Internet access. The Order is limited to facilities-based broadband Internet access service providers and VoIP providers that offer services that use the public switched telephone network ("interconnected VoIP providers).

In May 2006, the FCC addressed several outstanding issues regarding CALEA implementation. Among other clarifications, the FCC (1) affirmed its May 14, 2007 compliance deadline for facilities-based broadband Internet access and interconnected VoIP services, and clarified that the date applied to all such providers; (2) explained that the FCC does not plan to intervene in the standards-setting process in this matter; (3) permitted telecommunications carriers the option of using Trusted Third Parties to assist in meeting their CALEA obligations; (4) restricted the availability of compliance extensions to equipment, facilities, and services deployed prior to October 25, 1998; (5) found that the FCC may enforce action under section 229(a) of the Communications Act against carriers that fail to comply with CALEA; and (6) concluded that carriers are responsible for CALEA development and implementation costs for post-January 1, 1995, equipment and facilities, and declined to adopt a national surcharge to recover CALEA costs.

In June 2006, the United States Court of Appeals for the District of Columbia Circuit affirmed the FCC's decision concluding that VoIP and facilities-based broadband Internet access providers have CALEA obligations similar to those of telephone companies.

BACKGROUND

In the early 1 990s the Federal Bureau of Investigation (FBI) asked Congress for legislation to assist law enforcement agencies to continue conducting electronic surveillance. The FBI argued that the deployment of digital technologies in public telephone systems was making it increasingly difficult for law enforcement agencies to conduct electronic surveillance of communications over public telephone networks. As a result of these arguments and concerns from the telecommunications industry,[1] as well as issues raised by groups advocating protection of privacy rights,[2] the Communications Assistance for Law Enforcement Act (CALEA) was enacted on October 25, 1994 (47 U.S.C. 1001-1021), in the final days of the 103rd Congress.

CALEA is intended to preserve the ability of law enforcement officials to conduct electronic surveillance effectively and efficiently, despite the deployment of new digital technologies and wireless services by the telecommunications industry. CALEA requires telecommunications carriers to modify their equipment, facilities, and services to ensure that they are able to comply with authorized electronic surveillance. These modifications were originally planned to be completed by October 25, 1998. Since that time, the Federal Communications Commission (FCC) issued two additional orders establishing June 30, 2002, as the date by which telecommunications carries must have upgraded all their systems.[3] Equipment manufacturers have fulfilled their obligation to provide CALEA solutions and carriers are implementing them. The FBI and FCC continue to monitor and review the implementation of this program.

Some Technical Terms

As a result of the revolution in digital technology in telecommunications, the process of wiretapping and other electronic surveillance has become more complex, and legal ambiguities have been introduced. As a background to understanding the problems associated with CALEA implementation, the definitions of several terms are necessary. Electronic surveillance refers to either the interception of communications content (as in a conversation) also known as wiretapping, or the acquisition of call-identifying information (the number dialed). The latter activity is accomplished through the use of pen register devices, which capture call-identifying information for numbers of outgoing calls from the location of lawful interception, and traps and traces, which capture information for numbers received at the location of lawful interception, much like consumer caller ID systems. Under current federal law, law enforcement (i.e., police or the FBI) must obtain a court order before conducting any of these activities. However, a wiretap requires a higher "evidentiary burden" than a pen register or trap and trace, including showing that there is probable cause for believing that a person is committing one of a list of specific crimes.[4]

Under traditional analog technology, it was easy to separate the above categories of electronic surveillance. However, the advent of digital signal transmission technologies has made that distinction less clear. Information signals (voice or data) can be transmitted over telephone networks in one of two ways: circuit-switched and packet-switched modes.[5] In circuit-switched systems, a communications path is established between the parties and dedicated exclusively to one conversation for the duration of the call. In packet-switched systems, the information is broken down into smaller pieces called "packets"using a digital process. Each packet contains a small part of the message content along with call-identifying information called a "header" that indicates the origination and destination points of the information. Each packet is transmitted separately and is reassembled into the complete message at the destination point.

The packet-switched mode is the signal transmission technology used in all Internet communications. Packet switching is considered a more efficient use of a network than circuit switching because the same line can be used for multiple communications simultaneously. Although the circuit-switched mode was historically used in all voice telephone calls, the packet-switched mode is increasingly being used for voice and data transmissions over telephone networks.

CALEA'S MAIN PROVISIONS

CALEA requires telecommunications carriers to assist law enforcement in performing electronic surveillance on their digital networks pursuant to court order or other lawful authorization. The telecommunications industry, privacy rights groups, and law enforcement agencies agree that CALEA was not intended to expand law enforcement's authority to conduct electronic surveillance. On the contrary, CALEA was intended only to ensure that after law enforcement obtains the appropriate legal authority, carriers will have the necessary capabilities and sufficient capacity to assist law enforcement in conducting digital electronic surveillance regardless of the specific telecommunications systems or services deployed.

CALEA (47 U.S.C. 1002) directs the telecommunications industry to design, develop, and deploy solutions that meet certain assistance capability requirements for telecommunications carriers to support law enforcement in the conduct of lawfully-authorized electronic surveillance. Pursuant to a court order or other lawful authorization, carriers must be able, within certain limitations, to: (1) expeditiously isolate all wire and electronic communications of a target transmitted by the carrier within its service area; (2) expeditiously isolate call-identifying information that is reasonably available on a target; (3) provide intercepted communications and call-identifying information to law enforcement; and (4) carry out intercepts unobtrusively, so targets are not made aware of the electronic surveillance, and in a manner that does not compromise the privacy and security of other communications.

To allow carriers to give law enforcement the means to conduct its wiretaps, CALEA (47 U.S.C. 1003) requires the Attorney General to determine the number of simultaneous interceptions (law enforcement agencies' estimate of their *maximum capacity* requirements) that telecommunications carriers must be able to support.

To maintain privacy rights of individuals, CALEA (47 U.S.C. 1004) requires telecommunications carriers to ensure that any interception of communications or access to call-identifying information that is conducted within their premises can only be done with a court order. It also requires the specific intervention of an officer or employee of the carrier acting in accordance with regulations prescribed by the Federal Communications Commission (FCC).

CALEA (47 U.S.C. 1005) directs telecommunications carriers to consult with telecommunications equipment manufacturers to develop equipment necessary to comply with the capability and capacity requirements identified by the FBI. For efficient industry-wide implementation of the above requirements, CALEA (47 U.S.C. 1006) directs the law enforcement community to coordinate with the telecommunications industry and state utility commissions to develop suitable technical standards and establish compliance dates for equipment. In its *Eighth Annual Report*, the FBI stated that, "to date, most manufacturers have either complete, or nearly complete, CALEA solutions available for their carrier customers."[6]

CALEA (47 U.S.C. 1008) gives the Attorney General, subject to the availability of appropriations, authority to pay telecommunications carriers for all reasonable costs directly associated with the modifications performed by carriers in connection with equipment, facilities, and services installed or deployed on or before January 1, 1995 (known as the "grandfather" date).

MAJOR EVENTS FOLLOWING ENACTMENT OF CALEA

Initial Delays

CALEA gave implementation responsibility to the Attorney General, who, in turn, delegated the responsibility to the FBI. The FBI leads that nationwide effort on behalf of federal, state, and local law enforcement agencies. FBI officials initially anticipated that it would take a year for a standard to be developed and agreed upon by law enforcement, the telecommunications carriers, and the equipment manufacturers. Telecommunications consultants estimated that it would take the industry another three years to design, build and deploy new systems to comply with CALEA. Instead, industry and law enforcement became involved in a protracted dispute over what should be required for law enforcement's wiretapping capabilities.

By March 1997, the completion of the capability standard was overdue by 16 months. The FBI attempted to expedite the industry's implementation of CALEA by releasing regulations that included a cost recovery plan for the federal government's payment of costs associated with CALEA, as well as capability and capacity requirements for the industry to meet. The plan required more extensive upgrades to networks than the telecommunications industry believed were necessary for law enforcement to preserve its wiretapping capabilities. Industry groups and privacy advocates disputed the FBI's plan. They argued that the FBI was attempting to expand its surveillance capabilities beyond the congressional intention of CALEA, and was attempting to unfairly shift costs and accountability away from the federal government onto private industry. Furthermore, the industry argued that, without an adopted capability standard, it could not begin designing, manufacturing, and purchasing the equipment to achieve CALEA compliance.

In December 1997, the Telecommunications Industry Association (TIA, representing telecommunications equipment manufacturers) adopted, over the objections of the law enforcement community, a technical standard, J-STD-025, also known as the "J-standard." This standard prescribes upgrades to network devices to meet CALEA's assistance capability requirements for local exchange, cellular, and broadband personal communications services (PC S). Although the FBI claimed that the J-standard did not provide all of the capabilities needed, the industry asserted that CALEA's language stated that telecommunications carriers would be compliant if they met publicly available standards adopted by the industry.

Privacy rights groups, on the other hand, protested two aspects of the J- standard that they asserted would make information beyond what is legally required available to law enforcement. One was a feature enabling the telecommunications network to provide location information for users of mobile wireless telecommunications services. The location information protocols in J-STD-025 allow law enforcement agencies to obtain information on the physical location of the nearest cell site (i.e., the receiver/transmitter antenna and base station) of mobile phone handsets at the beginning and end of each call. Wireless carriers are now deploying another technology (called triangulation) that will enable the carriers, and law enforcement, to track wireless telephone users more precisely, potentially within a few meters. The other was a feature enabling the network to access packet-mode data from telephone calls using more advanced systems. Privacy rights groups argued that these capabilities would violate the Fourth Amendment rights of individuals against unreasonable searches and seizures. Despite these objections, telecommunications manufacturers began designing new switches and upgrades to existing switches according to the J-standard.

Currently, equipment manufacturers have successfully incorporated the J-standard into their new equipment and carriers are now well underway with their efforts to upgrade their systems.

The FBI's "Punch List"

In the negotiations to develop the J-standard, TIA had refused to include some of the capabilities that law enforcement officials claimed they needed to facilitate digital wiretapping. As a result, in March 1998, the FBI petitioned the FCC to require the telecommunications industry to adopt eleven additional capabilities. Industry and privacy rights groups protested that the FBI's plan would unlawfully expand enforcement capabilities. Eventually, the "punch-list"[7] included the following six[8] items:

- Content of subject-initiated conference calls — Would enable law enforcement to access the content of conference calls supported by the subject's service (including the call content of parties on hold).
- Party hold, join, drop — Messages would be sent to law enforcement that identify the active parties of a call. Specifically, on a conference call, these messages would indicate whether a party is on hold, has joined or has been dropped from the conference call.
- Subject-initiated dialing and signaling information — Access to all dialing and signaling information available from the subject would inform law enforcement of a subject's use of features (such as the use of flash-hook and other feature keys).
- In-band and out-of-band signaling (notification message) — A message would be sent to law enforcement whenever a subject's *service* sends a tone or other network message to the subject or associate (e.g., notification that a line is ringing or busy).
- Timing information — Information necessary to correlate call-identifying information with the call content of a communications interception.
- Dialed digit extraction — Information would include those digits dialed by a subject after the initial call setup is completed.[9]

Capacity Requirements

The FBI's subsequent implementation actions were also opposed by the telecommunications industry. In March 1998, the FBI announced its estimated capacity requirements for local exchange, cellular, and broadband PCS.[10] The industry protested the FBI's estimates, arguing that it would require telephone carriers to accommodate thousands of wiretaps simultaneously, an impractical and unnecessary burden. In July 1998, the FBI developed guidelines and procedures to facilitate small carrier compliance with its capacity requirements, and asked carriers to identify any systems or services that did not have the capacity to accommodate those requirements. In December 1998, the FBI began a proceeding to develop capacity requirements for services other than local exchange, cellular, and broadband PCS, asked additional questions of interested parties in June 2000.[11] These technologies and services included paging, mobile satellite services, specialized mobile radio, and enhanced specialized mobile radio. To date, the proceeding is still pending.

Previous FCC Actions

As a result of petitions from the industry and the FBI, the FCC became involved in the implementation of CALEA. In October 1997, the FCC released its first Notice of Proposed Rule Making (NPRM) on CALEA implementation.[12] The NPRM sought comments from interested parties regarding a set of policies and procedures proposed by the FCC for telecommunications carriers to follow. The proposed procedures would (1) preclude the unlawful interception of communications, (2) ensure that authorized interceptions are performed, (3) maintain secure and adequate records of any interceptions, and (4) determine what entities should be subject to these requirements, whether the requirements are reasonable, and whether to grant extensions of time for compliance with the requirements.

In response to the NPRM, telecommunications carriers, privacy rights groups, and the FBI submitted comments to the FCC to attempt to influence the final decision. Then, in April 1998, the FCC released a Public Notice requesting comments on issues raised in those petitions concerning the dates that carriers were required to comply with CALEA and the dispute over the J-standard. Based on comments it received, the FCC extended the implementation deadline until June 30, 2000, stating that without a standard, the necessary equipment would not be available in time.[13]

In October 1998, the FCC initiated a proceeding to review the technical capabilities prescribed by the J-standard.[14] The goal of that proceeding was to determine whether telecommunications carriers should be required under CALEA to meet the FBI's "punch list" items. The FCC addressed these issues in several documents released over the following year. In March 1999, the FCC's First Report and Order established the minimum capability requirements for telecommunications carriers to comply with CALEA.[15] Telecommunications carriers were required to ensure that only lawful wiretaps occur on their premises and that the occurrence of wiretaps is not divulged to anyone other than authorized law enforcement personnel. On August 2, 1999, the FCC decided to allow carriers to decide how long they would maintain their records of law enforcement's wiretap, pen register, and trap and trace interceptions.[16] On August 31, 1999, the Second Report and Order established a definition for "telecommunications carrier" to include all common carriers, cable operators, electric and other utilities that offer telecommunications services to the public, commercial mobile radio services, and service resellers.[17] The definition did not include Internet service providers (ISPs), which were explicitly excluded under the CALEA statute.

The FCC's Third Report and Order, released August 31, 1999, adopted technical requirements for wireline, cellular, and broadband PCS carriers to comply with CALEA requirements.[18] The ruling adopted the J-standard, including the two capabilities that were opposed by the privacy rights groups (i.e., the ability to provide location information and packet-mode data to law enforcement). As described above, the FCC also adopted six of the punch list capabilities requested by the FBI to be implemented by telecommunications carriers. The Order required all aspects of the J-standard except for the packet-mode data collection capability to be implemented by June 30, 2000. The Order required carriers to comply with the packet-mode data capability and the six punch list capabilities by September 30, 2001.[19] (The FCC ultimately extended the date by which all telecommunications carriers must have upgraded their systems to June 30, 2002.[20])

On April 9, 2001, the FCC adopted its Second Order on Reconsideration,[21] which clarified the arrangements telecommunications carriers must make to ensure that law enforcement agencies can contact them when necessary, and the interception activity that triggers a record-keeping requirement.

In September 2001, FCC released a tandem Order[22] and Public Notice[23] on CALEA implementation. In the Order, the Commission extended until November 19, 2001, the deadline by which wireline, cellular, and broadband personal communications services (PC S) carriers must implement a packet-mode communications electronic surveillance capability, or to seek individual relief under section 107(c) of CALEA. The notice explained the petitioning process for telecommunications carriers seeking relief under section 107(c) for an extension of the new compliance deadline with respect to packet-mode communications, as well as other safe harbor standards.

Finally, on April 11, 2002, the FCC released an Order on Remand,[24] which responded to a decision issued by the United States Court of Appeals for the District of Columbia Circuit[25] vacating four of the punch list electronic surveillance capabilities mandated by the Third Report and Order in this proceeding. The FCC found that all of the capabilities were necessary and authorized by CALEA and had to be provided by wireline, cellular, and broadband PCS telecommunications carriers by June 30, 2002. The FCC also required that two additional punch list capabilities that were mandated by the Third Report and Order, but not reviewed by the Court of Appeals be provided by that same date.

The FCC granted preliminary extensions to requesting carriers with respect to punch list implementation that will expire on June 30, 2004. It granted preliminary extensions in connection with "packet" services that had been scheduled to expire on November 19, 2003, but that date was further extended to January 30, 2004. No further action with respect to that extension has been taken.

GOVERNMENT ACTIVITY: 2004 – PRESENT

The FBI and other law enforcement agencies, the FCC, and Congress are all concerned with CALEA-related issues, particularly with respect to packet-based services (i.e., voice over Internet Protocol [VoIP]) and "push-to-talk" services offered by wireless providers.

FBI Activity

The FBI has remained active in promoting its positions related to its CALEA powers.

Comments to the FCC's Wireless Broadband Task Force Report

On April 22, 2005, the Department of Justice (DOJ) filed comments on the FCC's Wireless Broadband Task Force Report,[26] requesting that the FCC "continue to preserve the vital national security and criminal law enforcement capabilities of CALEA as it develops a deregulatory framework for wireless broadband Internet access services." Reply comments in the proceeding were due May 23, 2005.

Notice of Information Collection under Review

On April 13, 2005, the FBI published a 60-day Notice of Information Collection Under Review.[27] The notice announced a CALEA Readiness Survey program, which seeks to evaluate the effectiveness of CIU programs for implementing CALEA solutions in the Public Switched Telephone Network. Comments in this proceeding were accepted until June 13, 2005.

Petition for Declaratory Ruling

On March 10, 2004, the FBI, the DOJ, and the Drug Enforcement Administration petitioned the FCC to identify additional telecommunications services not identified specifically within CALEA that should be subject to it.[28] The services named in the FBI petition include some now considered beyond the scope of CALEA by many observers, including services that fall under the FCC's definition of "information services" under the Communications Act of 1934. However, CALEA provides the FCC a broader framework to determine that a service is a "telecommunications service." Comments and replies to the petition were due April 12 and April 27, 2004, respectively. The FCC ruled on this Petition on August 5, 2005, discussed below (See "FCC Action," page 10).

Inspector General Report

The FBI's Inspector General issued a report in April 2004 on CALEA implementation.[29] In its report, the IG expressed concern over the cost estimates for obtaining CALEA compliance, which have varied widely. Industry has stated it believes estimates full compliance will cost approximately $1.3 billion; the FBI has estimated costs in the range of $500 million to $1 billion. Further, in December 2003, the FBI estimated that an additional $204 million would be necessary to complete deployment of CALEA. The IG stated in its report that it did not believe implementation costs could be determined with any degree of specificity, but that it was unlikely CALEA could be implemented with the $49.5 million that remains unobligated from current funding.

FCC Activity

In response to law enforcement's petition and after considering the comments and replies from interested parties, the FCC released an NPRM and Declaratory Ruling on August 4, 2004.[30] Additionally, the FCC has issued two Orders in this matter.

Declaratory Ruling

In the Declaratory Ruling accompanying the NPRM, the FCC clarified that commercial wireless "push-to-talk" services are subject to CALEA, regardless of the technologies that wireless providers choose to apply in offering them.

First Report and Order

On August 5, 2005, the FCC ruled that providers of certain broadband and interconnected VoIP services must accommodate law enforcement wiretaps.[31] The FCC found that these services can be considered replacements for conventional telecommunications services currently subject to wiretap rules, including circuit-switched voice service and dial-up Internet access. As such, the new services are covered by CALEA, which requires the FCC to preserve the ability of law enforcement to conduct wiretaps as technology evolves. The rules are limited to facilities-based broadband Internet access service providers and VoIP providers that offer services permitting users to receive calls from, and place calls to, the public switched telephone network — these providers are called interconnected VoIP providers.

In making its ruling, the FCC found that the definition of "telecommunications carrier" in CALEA is broader than the definition of that term in the Communications Act and can, therefore, include providers of services that are not classified as telecommunications services under the Communications Act. CALEA contains a broader definition of telecommunications provider that authorizes the FCC to classify an entity a telecommunications carrier if it finds that such service is a replacement for a substantial portion of the local telephone exchange.

The FCC established a deadline of 18 months from the effective date of the Order for providers to achieve full compliance and adopted a Further Notice of Proposed Rulemaking to seek more information about whether specific classes of facilities-based broadband Internet access providers should be exempt from CALEA (i.e., small and rural providers and providers of broadband networks for educational and research institutions).

A coalition of organizations filed a Petition for Review with the United States Court of Appeals for the District of Columbia Circuit on October 25, 2005.[32] Specifically, the "petitioners seek relief from the Order on the grounds that it exceeds the Commission's statutory authority and is arbitrary, capricious, unsupported by substantial evidence, and contrary to law. Petitioners request that this Court vacate the Order and the Final Rules adopted therein and grant such other relief as may be appropriate."[33]

Second Report and Order

On May 3, 2006,[34] the FCC addressed several issues regarding CALEA implementation, specifically, the Order:

- Affirms the May 14, 2007, CALEA compliance deadline for facilities-based broadband Internet access and interconnected VoIP services (as established by the First Report and Order) and clarifies that the date will apply to all such providers.

- Explains that the FCC does not plan, at this time, to intervene in the standards-setting process in this matter.
- Permits telecommunications carriers the option of using Trusted Third Parties (TTPs) to assist in meeting their CALEA obligations.
- Restricts the availability of compliance extensions to equipment, facilities, and services deployed prior to October 25, 1998.
- Finds that the commission may, in addition to law enforcement remedies available through the courts, take separate enforcement action under section 229(a) of the Communications Act against carriers that fail to comply with CALEA.
- Concludes that carriers are responsible for CALEA development and implementation costs for post-January 1, 1995, equipment and facilities, and declines to adopt a national surcharge to recover CALEA costs.
- Requires all carriers providing facilities-based broadband Internet access and interconnected VoIP service to submit interim reports to the FCC to ensure that they will be CALEA-compliant by May 14, 2007, and also requires all such providers to which CALEA obligations were applied in the First Report and Order to come into compliance with the system security requirements in the commission's rules within 90 days of the effective date of this Second Report and Order.

Court Challenge

In June 2006, the United States Court of Appeals for the District of Columbia Circuit affirmed the FCC's decision concluding that VoIP and facilities-based broadband Internet access providers have CALEA obligations similar to those of telephone companies.[35]

Congressional Activity: 110th Congress

No bills have been introduced in the 1 10th Congress that would amend the CALEA statute.

REFERENCES

[1] In this report, the telecommunications industry includes common carrier telephone companies, mobile wireless telecommunications providers, telecommunications equipment manufacturers, and other entities that provide telecommunications services to the public.

[2] Privacy rights groups involved in the CALEA debate include the Electronic Privacy Information Center, the Electronic Frontier Foundation, advocacy groups which both support on-line privacy rights of individuals, the Center for Democracy and Technology, which also advocates electronic privacy (and is funded primarily by the telecommunications, computer, and media industries), and the American Civil Liberties Union (ACLU), which represents a broad array of civil rights based on the First and Fourth Amendments.

[3] United States Department of Justice, Federal Bureau of Investigation, *Communications Assistance for Law Enforcement Act, Eighth Annual Report to Congress*, November 30, 2002 (*Eighth Annual Report*), pp. 7-9.

[4] See CRS Report 98-326, *Privacy: An Overview of Federal Statutes Governing Wiretapping and Electronic Eavesdropping*, by Gina Stevens and Charles Doyle.

[5] Switches are network devices that select a path or circuit for sending data to its next destination over the telephone network. Switches may also include functions of the router, a device also used in computer networks, that determines the route and adjacent network point for data to be sent.

[6] Eighth Annual Report, p. 5.

[7] The "punch list" was named as such by the telecommunications industry, which believed the FBI was improperly forcing industry to comply with the FBI's requirements.

[8] The additional capabilities originally requested by the FBI that were not included were: standardized delivery interface; separated delivery, surveillance status; continuity check tone (c-tone); and feature status.

[9] *Federal Register* 63 page 63639, FCC, Further Notice of Proposed Rulemaking, November 16, 1998.

[10] *Federal Register* 63, page 12217, FBI, Final Notice of Capacity, March 12, 1998.

[11] *Federal Register* 63, page 70160, FBI Notice of Inquiry, December 18, 1998, and *Federal Register* 65, page 40694, FBI Further Notice of Inquiry, June 30, 2000.

[12] FCC NPRM CC Docket No. 97-213, FCC Record 97-356, released October 10, 1997.

[13] FCC Memorandum Opinion and Order in the Matter of Petition for the Extension of the Compliance Date under Section 107 of CALEA, released September 11, 1998.

[14] FCC Proposes Rules to Meet Technical Requirements of CALEA. Report No. ET 9 8-8. FCC News, October 22, 1998.

[15] FCC 99-11, Report and Order CC Docket No. 97-213, released March 15, 1999.

[16] FCC 99-184, Order on Reconsideration, CC Docket No. 97-213, released August 2, 1999.

[17] FCC 99-229, Second Report and Order, CC Docket No. 97-213, released August 31, 1999.

[18] FCC 99-230, Third Report and Order, CC Docket No. 97-213, released August 31, 1999.

[19] FCC Sides with FBI on Tapping, *Wired News*, August 27, 1999, [http://www.wired.com/news].

[20] FCC Pubic Notice DA 02-270, released March 26, 2002.

[21] *Federal Register* 66, page 22446, FCC, Second Order on Reconsideration, CC Docket No. 97-213, May 4, 2001.

[22] *Federal Register* 66, page 50841, FCC, Order, CC Docket No. 97-213, October 5, 2001.

[23] FCC Pubic Notice DA 01-2243, released September 28, 2001.

[24] *Federal Register* 67, page 21999, Order on Remand, CC Docket No. 97-213, May 2, 2002.

[25] See United States Telecom. Association v. FCC, 227 F.3d 450 (D.C. Cir. 2000), available at [http://www.fcc.gov/ogc/documents/opinions/2000/99-1442.html].

[26] GN Docket No. 04-163. Additional information on this topic can be found online at the FCC's website at [http://www.fcc.gov/wbatf].

[27] 70 *Fed. Reg.* 19,503 (2005). This document is available online at [http://www.askcalea.net/docs/20050413_70fr19503.pdf].

[28] Joint Petition for Expedited Rulemaking of United States Department of Justice, Federal Bureau of Investigation, and Drug Enforcement Administration, RM-10865, March 10, 2004.

[29] U.S. Department of Justice, Office of the Inspector General of the, entitled "Implementation of the Communications Assistance for Law Enforcement Act by the Federal Bureau of Investigation," available at [http://www.usdoj .gov/oig/reports/FBI/ a0419/index.htm], April 7, 2004.

[30] *In the Matter of Communications Assistance for Law Enforcement Act and Broadband Access and Services, Notice of Proposed Rulemaking and Declaratory Ruling*, FCC 04-187, ET Docket 04-295, RM-10865, adopted August 4, 2004, released August 9, 2004. Available online at [http://hraunfoss.fcc.gov/edocs_public/attachmatch/F CC-04-1 87A1 .pdf]. See also Federal Register 69, page 56976.

[31] *In the Matter of Communications Assistance for Law Enforcement Act and Broadband Access and Services, First Report and Order and Further Notice of Proposed Rulemaking*, FCC 05-153, ET Docket 04-295, RM-10865, adopted August 5, 2005, released September 23, 2005. Available online at [http://hraunfoss.fcc.gov/edocs_public/attachmatch/ FCC-05-1 53A1 .pdf].

[32] The coalition is composed of CompTel, American Library Association, Association of Research Libraries, Center for Democracy & Technology, Electronic Frontier Foundation, Electronic Privacy Information Center, Pulver.com, and Sun Microsystems.

[33] A copy of the Petition, No. 05-1408, is available online at [http://www.cdt.org/ digi_tele/2005 1 025 caleapetition.pdf].

[34] *In the Matter of Communications Assistance for Law Enforcement Act and Broadband Access and Services, Second Report and Order and Memorandum Opinion and Order*, FCC 06-56, ET Docket 04-295, adopted May 3, 2006. This Order has not yet been released, but the news release is available online at [http://hraunfoss.fcc.gov/edocs_public/ attachmatch/DOC-26522 1A1 .pdf].

[35] American Council on Education v. FCC, No. 05-1404 (Consolidated with 05-1408, 05-1438, 05-1451, 05-1453). Argued May 5, 2006; decided June 9, 2006. Available online at [http://hraunfoss.fcc.gov/edocs_public/ attachmatch/DOC-266204A1 .pdf].

In: Digital Surveillance
Editor: J. G. Massingale, pp. 17-64

ISBN: 978-1-60692-312-2

Chapter 2

DATA MINING AND HOMELAND SECURITY: AN OVERVIEW*

Jeffrey W. Seifert

ABSTRACT

Data mining has become one of the key features of many homeland security initiatives. Often used as a means for detecting fraud, assessing risk, and product retailing, data mining involves the use of data analysis tools to discover previously unknown, valid patterns and relationships in large data sets. In the context of homeland security, data mining can be a potential means to identify terrorist activities, such as money transfers and communications, and to identify and track individual terrorists themselves, such as through travel and immigration records.

While data mining represents a significant advance in the type of analytical tools currently available, there are limitations to its capability. One limitation is that although data mining can help reveal patterns and relationships, it does not tell the user the value or significance of these patterns. These types of determinations must be made by the user. A second limitation is that while data mining can identify connections between behaviors and/or variables, it does not necessarily identify a causal relationship. Successful data mining still requires skilled technical and analytical specialists who can structure the analysis and interpret the output.

---

* This is an edited, excerpted and augmented edition of a Congressional Research Service publication, Report RL31798, dated April 3, 2008.

Data mining is becoming increasingly common in both the private and public sectors. Industries such as banking, insurance, medicine, and retailing commonly use data mining to reduce costs, enhance research, and increase sales. In the public sector, data mining applications initially were used as a means to detect fraud and waste, but have grown to also be used for purposes such as measuring and improving program performance. However, some of the homeland security data mining applications represent a significant expansion in the quantity and scope of data to be analyzed. Some efforts that have attracted a higher level of congressional interest include the Terrorism Information Awareness (TIA) project (now-discontinued) and the Computer-Assisted Passenger Prescreening System II (CAPPS II) project (now- canceled and replaced by Secure Flight). Other initiatives that have been the subject of congressional interest include the Multi-State Anti-Terrorism Information Exchange (MATRIX), the Able Danger program, the Automated Targeting System (ATS), and data collection and analysis projects being conducted by the National Security Agency (NSA).

As with other aspects of data mining, while technological capabilities are important, there are other implementation and oversight issues that can influence the success of a project's outcome. One issue is data quality, which refers to the accuracy and completeness of the data being analyzed. A second issue is the interoperability of the data mining software and databases being used by different agencies. A third issue is mission creep, or the use of data for purposes other than for which the data were originally collected. A fourth issue is privacy. Questions that may be considered include the degree to which government agencies should use and mix commercial data with government data, whether data sources are being used for purposes other than those for which they were originally designed, and possible application of the Privacy Act to these initiatives. It is anticipated that congressional oversight of data mining projects will grow as data mining efforts continue to evolve.

WHAT IS DATA MINING?

Data mining involves the use of sophisticated data analysis tools to discover previously unknown, valid patterns and relationships in large data sets.[1] These tools can include statistical models, mathematical algorithms, and machine learning methods (algorithms that improve their performance automatically through experience, such as neural networks or decision trees). Consequently, data mining consists of more than collecting and managing data, it also includes analysis and prediction.

Data mining can be performed on data represented in quantitative, textual, or multimedia forms. Data mining applications can use a variety of parameters to examine the data. They include association (patterns where one event is connected to another event, such as purchasing a pen and purchasing paper), sequence or path analysis (patterns where one event leads to another event, such as the birth of a child and purchasing diapers), classification (identification of new patterns, such as coincidences between duct tape purchases and plastic sheeting purchases), clustering (finding and visually documenting groups of previously unknown facts, such as geographic location and brand preferences), and forecasting (discovering patterns from which one can make reasonable predictions regarding future activities, such as the prediction that people who join an athletic club may take exercise classes).[2]

As an application, compared to other data analysis applications, such as structured queries (used in many commercial databases) or statistical analysis software, data mining represents a *difference of kind rather than degree*. Many simpler analytical tools utilize a verification-based approach, where the user develops a hypothesis and then tests the data to prove or disprove the hypothesis. For example, a user might hypothesize that a customer who buys a hammer, will also buy a box of nails. The effectiveness of this approach can be limited by the creativity of the user to develop various hypotheses, as well as the structure of the software being used. In contrast, data mining utilizes a discovery approach, in which algorithms can be used to examine several multidimensional data relationships simultaneously, identifying those that are unique or frequently represented. For example, a hardware store may compare their customers' tool purchases with home ownership, type of automobile driven, age, occupation, income, and/or distance between residence and the store. As a result of its complex capabilities, two precursors are important for a successful data mining exercise; a clear formulation of the problem to be solved, and access to the relevant data.[3]

Reflecting this conceptualization of data mining, some observers consider data mining to be just one step in a larger process known as knowledge discovery in databases (KDD). Other steps in the KDD process, in progressive order, include data cleaning, data integration, data selection, data transformation, (data mining), pattern evaluation, and knowledge presentation.[4]

A number of advances in technology and business processes have contributed to a growing interest in data mining in both the public and private sectors. Some of these changes include the growth of computer networks, which can be used to connect databases; the development of enhanced search-related techniques such as neural networks and advanced algorithms; the spread of the client/server computing model, allowing users to access centralized data resources from the desktop; and an increased ability to combine data from disparate sources into a single searchable source.[5]

In addition to these improved data management tools, the increased availability of information and the decreasing costs of storing it have also played a role. Over the past several years there has been a rapid increase in the volume of information collected and stored, with some observers suggesting that the quantity of the world's data approximately doubles every year.[6] At the same time, the costs of data storage have decreased significantly from dollars per megabyte to pennies per megabyte. Similarly, computing power has continued to double every 18-24 months, while the relative cost of computing power has continued to decrease.[7]

Data mining has become increasingly common in both the public and private sectors. Organizations use data mining as a tool to survey customer information, reduce fraud and waste, and assist in medical research. However, the proliferation of data mining has raised some implementation and oversight issues as well. These include concerns about the quality of the data being analyzed, the interoperability of the databases and software between agencies, and potential infringements on privacy. Also, there are some concerns that the limitations of data mining are being overlooked as agencies work to emphasize their homeland security initiatives.

Limitations of Data Mining as a Terrorist Detection Tool

While data mining products can be very powerful tools, they are not self-sufficient applications. To be successful, data mining requires skilled technical and analytical specialists who can structure the analysis and interpret the output that is created. Consequently, the limitations of data mining are primarily data or personnel-related, rather than technology-related.[8]

Although data mining can help reveal patterns and relationships, it does not tell the user the value or significance of these patterns. These types of determinations must be made by the user. Similarly, the validity of the patterns discovered is dependent on how they compare to "real world" circumstances. For example, to assess the validity of a data mining application designed to identify potential terrorist suspects in a large pool of individuals, the user may test the model using data that includes information about known terrorists. However, while possibly re-affirming a particular profile, it does not necessarily mean that the application will identify a suspect whose behavior significantly deviates from the original model.

Another limitation of data mining is that while it can identify connections between behaviors and/or variables, it does not necessarily identify a causal relationship. For example, an application may identify that a pattern of behavior, such as the propensity to purchase airline tickets just shortly before the flight is scheduled to depart, is related to characteristics such as income, level of education, and Internet use. However, that does not necessarily indicate that the ticket purchasing behavior is caused by one or more of these variables. In fact, the individual's behavior could be affected by some additional variable(s) such as occupation (the need to make trips on short notice), family status (a sick relative needing care), or a hobby (taking advantage of last minute discounts to visit new destinations).[9]

Beyond these specific limitations, some researchers suggest that the circumstances surrounding our knowledge of terrorism make data mining an ill-suited tool for identifying (predicting) potential terrorists before an activity occurs. Successful "predictive data mining" requires a significant number of known instances of a particular behavior in order to develop valid predictive models. For example, data mining used to predict types of consumer behavior (i.e., the likelihood of someone shopping at a particular store, the potential of a credit card usage being fraudulent) may be based on as many as millions of previous instances of the same particular behavior. Moreover, such a robust data set can still lead to false positives. In contrast, as a CATO Institute report suggests that the relatively small number of terrorist incidents or attempts each year are too few and individually unique "to enable the creation of valid predictive models."[10]

DATA MINING USES

Data mining is used for a variety of purposes in both the private and public sectors. Industries such as banking, insurance, medicine, and retailing commonly use data mining to reduce costs, enhance research, and increase sales. For example, the insurance and banking industries use data mining applications to detect fraud and assist in risk assessment (e.g., credit scoring). Using customer data collected over several years, companies can develop models that predict whether a customer is a good credit risk, or whether an accident claim may be fraudulent and should be investigated more closely. The medical community sometimes uses data mining to help predict the effectiveness of a procedure or medicine. Pharmaceutical firms use data mining of chemical compounds and genetic material to help guide research on new treatments for diseases. Retailers can use information collected through affinity programs (e.g., shoppers' club cards, frequent flyer points, contests) to assess the effectiveness of product selection and placement decisions, coupon offers, and which products are often purchased together. Companies such as telephone service providers and music clubs can use data mining to create a "churn analysis," to assess which customers are likely to remain as subscribers and which ones are likely to switch to a competitor.[11]

In the public sector, data mining applications were initially used as a means to detect fraud and waste, but they have grown also to be used for purposes such as measuring and improving program performance. It has been reported that data mining has helped the federal government recover millions of dollars in fraudulent Medicare payments.[12] The Justice Department has been able to use data mining to assess crime patterns and adjust resource allotments accordingly. Similarly, the Department of Veterans Affairs has used data mining to help predict demographic changes in the constituency it serves so that it can better estimate its budgetary needs. Another example is the Federal Aviation Administration, which uses data mining to review plane crash data to recognize common defects and recommend precautionary measures.[13]

In addition, data mining has been increasingly cited as an important tool for homeland security efforts. Some observers suggest that data mining should be used as a means to identify terrorist activities, such as money transfers and communications, and to identify and track individual terrorists themselves, such as through travel and immigration records. Initiatives that have attracted significant attention include the now-discontinued Terrorism Information Awareness (TIA) project[14] conducted by the Defense Advanced Research Projects Agency (DARPA), and the now-canceled Computer-Assisted Passenger Prescreening System II (CAPPS II) that was being developed by the Transportation Security Administration (TSA). CAPPS II is being replaced by a new program called Secure Flight. Other initiatives that have been the subject of congressional interest include the Able Danger program and data collection and analysis projects being conducted by the National Security Agency (NSA).

Terrorism Information Awareness (TIA) Program

In the immediate aftermath of the September 11, 2001, terrorist attacks, many questions were raised about the country's intelligence tools and capabilities, as well as the government's ability to detect other so-called "sleeper cells," if, indeed, they existed. One response to these concerns was the creation of the Information Awareness Office (IAO) at the Defense Advanced Research Projects Agency (DARPA)[15] in January 2002. The role of IAO was "in part to bring together, under the leadership of one technical office director, several existing DARPA programs focused on applying information technology to combat terrorist threats."[16] The mission statement for IAO suggested that the emphasis on these technology programs was to "counter asymmetric threats by achieving *total information awareness* useful for preemption, national security warning, and national security decision making."[17] To that end, the TIA project was to focus on three specific areas of research, anticipated to be conducted over five years, to develop technologies that would assist in the detection of terrorist groups planning attacks against American interests, both inside and outside the country. The three areas of research and their purposes were described in a DOD Inspector General report as:

> ... language translation, data search with pattern recognition and privacy protection, and advanced collaborative and decision support tools. Language translation technology would enable the rapid analysis of foreign languages, both spoken and written, and allow analysts to quickly search the translated materials for clues about emerging threats. The data search, pattern recognition, and privacy protection technologies would permit analysts to search vast quantities of data for patterns that suggest terrorist activity while at the same time controlling access to the data, enforcing laws and policies, and ensuring detection of misuse of the information obtained. The collaborative reasoning and decision support technologies would allow analysts from different agencies to share data. [18]

Each part had the potential to improve the data mining capabilities of agencies that adopt the technology.[19] Automated rapid language translation could allow analysts to search and monitor foreign language documents and transmissions more quickly than currently possible. Improved search and pattern recognition technologies may enable more comprehensive and thorough mining of transactional data, such as passport and visa applications, car rentals, driver license renewals, criminal records, and airline ticket purchases. Improved collaboration and decision support tools might facilitate the search and coordination activities being conducted by different agencies and levels of government.[20]

In public statements DARPA frequently referred to the TIA program as a research and development project designed to create experimental prototype tools, and that the research agency would only use "data that is legally available and obtainable by the U.S. Government."[21] DARPA further emphasized that these tools could be adopted and used by *other* agencies, and that DARPA itself would not be engaging in any actual-use data mining applications, although it could "support production of a scalable leave-behind system prototype."[22] In addition, some of the technology projects being carried out in association with the TIA program did not involve data mining.[23] However, the TIA program's overall emphasis on collecting, tracking, and analyzing data trails left by individuals served to generate significant and vocal opposition soon after John Poindexter made a presentation on TIA at the DARPATech 2002 Conference in August 2002.[24]

Critics of the TIA program were further incensed by two administrative aspects of the project. The first involved the Director of IAO, Dr. John M. Poindexter. Poindexter, a retired Admiral, was, until that time, perhaps most well-known for his alleged role in the Iran-contra scandal during the Reagan Administration. His involvement with the program caused many in the civil liberties community to question the true motives behind TIA.[25] The second source of contention involved TIA's original logo, which depicted an "all-seeing" eye atop of a pyramid looking down over the globe, accompanied by the Latin phrase *scientia est potentia* (knowledge is power).[26] Although DARPA eventually removed the logo from its website, it left a lasting impression.

The continued negative publicity surrounding the TIA program contributed to the introduction of a number of bills in Congress that eventually led to the program's dissolution. Among these bills was S. 188, the Data-Mining Moratorium Act of 2003, which, if passed, would have imposed a moratorium on the implementation of data mining under the TIA program by the Department of Defense, as well as any similar program by the Department of Homeland Security. An amendment included in the Omnibus Appropriations Act for Fiscal Year 2003 (P.L. 108-7) required the Director of Central Intelligence, the Secretary of Defense, and the Attorney General to submit a joint report to Congress within 90 days providing details about the TIA program.[27] Funding for TIA as a whole was prohibited with the passage of the FY2004 Department of Defense Appropriations Act (P.L. 108-87) in September 2003. However, Section 8131 of the law allowed unspecified subcomponents of the TIA initiative to be funded as part of DOD's classified budget, subject to the provisions of the National Foreign Intelligence Program, which restricts the processing and analysis of information on U.S. citizens.[28]

Computer-Assisted Passenger Prescreening System (CAPPS II)

Similar to TIA, the CAPPS II project represented a direct response to the September 11, 2001, terrorist attacks. With the images of airliners flying into buildings fresh in people's minds, air travel was now widely viewed not only as a critically vulnerable terrorist target, but also as a weapon for inflicting larger harm. The CAPPS II initiative was intended to replace the original CAPPS, currently being used. Spurred, in part, by the growing number of airplane bombings, the existing CAPPS (originally called CAPS) was developed through a grant provided by the Federal Aviation Administration (FAA) to Northwest Airlines, with a prototype system tested in 1996. In 1997, other major carriers also began work on screening systems, and, by 1998, most of the U.S.-based airlines had voluntarily implemented CAPS, with the remaining few working toward implementation.[29] Also, during this time, the White House Commission on Aviation Safety and Security (sometimes referred to as the Gore Commission) released its final report in February 1 997.[30] Included in the commission's report was a recommendation that the United States implement automated passenger profiling for its airports.[31] On April 19, 1999, the FAA issued a notice of proposed rulemaking (NPRM) regarding the security of checked baggage on flights within the United States (docket no. FAA-1999-5536).[32] As part of this still-pending rule, domestic flights would be required to utilize "the FAA-approved computer-assisted passenger screening (CAPS) system to select passengers whose checked baggage must be subjected to additional security measures."[33]

The current CAPPS system is a rule-based system that uses the information provided by the passenger when purchasing the ticket to determine if the passenger fits into one of two categories; "selectees" requiring additional security screening, and those who do not. CAPPS also compares the passenger name to those on a list of known or suspected terrorists.[34] CAPPS II was described by TSA as "an enhanced system to confirm the identities of passengers and to identify foreign terrorists or persons with terrorist connections before they can board U.S. aircraft."[35] CAPPS II would have sent information provided by the passenger in the passengers name record (PNR), including full name, address, phone number, and date of birth, to commercial data providers for comparison to authenticate the identity of the passenger. The commercial data provider would have then transmitted a numerical score back to TSA indicating a particular risk level.[36] Passengers with a "green" score would have undergone "normal screening," while passengers with a "yellow" score would have undergone additional screening. Passengers with a "red" score would not have been allowed to board the flight, and would have received "the attention of law enforcement."[37] While drawing on information from commercial databases, TSA had stated that it would not see the actual information used to calculate the scores, and that it would not retain the traveler's information.

TSA had planned to test the system at selected airports during spring 2004.[38] However, CAPPS II encountered a number of obstacles to implementation. One obstacle involved obtaining the required data to test the system. Several high-profile debacles resulting in class-action lawsuits have made the U.S.-based airlines very wary of voluntarily providing passenger information. In early 2003, Delta Airlines was to begin testing CAPPS II using its customers' passenger data at three airports across the country. However, Delta became the target of a vociferous boycott campaign, raising further concerns about CAPPS II generally.[39] In September 2003, it was revealed that JetBlue shared private passenger information in September 2002 with Torch Concepts, a defense contractor, which was testing a data mining application for the U.S. Army. The information shared reportedly included itineraries, names, addresses, and phone numbers for 1.5 million passengers.[40] In January 2004, it was reported that Northwest Airlines provided personal information on millions of its passengers to the National Aeronautics and Space Administration (NASA) from October to December 2001 for an airline security-related data mining experiment.[41] In April 2004, it was revealed that American Airlines agreed to provide private passenger data on 1.2 million of its customers to TSA in June 2002, although the information was sent instead to four companies competing to win a contract with TSA.[42] Further instances of data being provided for the purpose of testing CAPPS II were brought to light during a Senate Committee on Government Affairs confirmation hearing on June 23, 2004. In his answers to the committee, the acting director of TSA, David M. Stone, stated that during 2002 and 2003 four airlines; Delta, Continental, America West, and Frontier, and two travel reservation companies; Galileo International and Sabre Holdings, provided passenger records to TSA and/or its contractors.[43]

Concerns about privacy protections had also dissuaded the European Union (EU) from providing any data to TSA to test CAPPS II. However, in May 2004, the EU signed an agreement with the United States that would have allowed PNR data for flights originating from the EU to be used in testing CAPPS II, but only after TSA was authorized to use domestic data as well. As part of the agreement, the EU data was to be retained for only three-and-a-half years (unless it is part of a law enforcement action), only 34 of the 39 elements of the PNR were to be accessed by authorities,[44] and there were to be yearly joint DHS-EU reviews of the implementation of the agreement.[45]

Another obstacle was the perception of mission creep. CAPPS II was originally intended to just screen for high-risk passengers who may pose a threat to safe air travel. However, in an August 1, 2003, *Federal Register* notice, TSA stated that CAPPS II could also be used to identify individuals with outstanding state or federal arrest warrants, as well as identify both foreign *and* domestic terrorists (not just foreign terrorists). The notice also states that CAPPS II could be "linked with the U.S. Visitor and Immigrant Status Indicator Technology (US-VISIT) program" to identify individuals who are in the country illegally (e.g., individuals with expired visas, illegal aliens, etc.).[46] In response to critics who cited these possible uses as examples of mission creep, TSA claimed that the suggested uses were consistent with the goals of improving aviation security.[47]

Several other concerns had also been raised, including the length of time passenger information was to be retained, who would have access to the information, the accuracy of the commercial data being used to authenticate a passenger's identity, the creation of procedures to allow passengers the opportunity to correct data errors in their records, and the ability of the system to detect attempts by individuals to use identity theft to board a plane undetected.

Secure Flight

In August 2004, TSA announced that the CAPPS II program was being canceled and would be replaced with a new system called Secure Flight. In the Department of Homeland Security Appropriations Act, 2005 (P.L. 108-334), Congress included a provision (Sec. 522) prohibiting the use of appropriated funds for "deployment or implementation, on other than a test basis," of CAPPS II, Secure Flight, "or other follow on/successor programs," until GAO has certified that such a system has met all of the privacy requirements enumerated in a February 2004 GAO report,[48] can accommodate any unique air transportation needs as it relates to interstate transportation, and that "appropriate life-cycle cost estimates, and expenditure and program plans exist." GAO's certification report[49] was delivered to Congress in March 2005. In its report, GAO found that while "TSA is making progress in addressing key areas of congressional interest ... TSA has not yet completed these efforts or fully addressed these areas, due largely to the current stage of the program's development."[50] In follow-up reports in February 2006[51] and June 2006,[52] GAO reiterated that while TSA continued to make progress, the Secure Flight program still suffered from systems development and program management problems, preventing it from meeting its congressionally mandated privacy requirements. In early 2006 TSA suspended development of Secure Flight in order to "rebaseline" or reassess the program.

In December 2006, the DHS Privacy Office released a report comparing TSA's published privacy notices with its actual practices regarding Secure Flight. The DHS Privacy Office found that there were discrepancies related to data testing and retention, due in part because the privacy notices "were drafted before the testing program had been designed fully." However, the report also points out that

> material changes in a federal program's design that have an impact on the collection, use, and maintenance of personally identifiable information of American citizens are required to be announced in Privacy Act system notices and privacy impact assessments.[53]

In a February 2007 interview, it was reported that TSA Administrator Kip Hawley stated that while TSA has developed a means to improve the accuracy, privacy, and reliability of Secure Flight, it would take approximately one-and-a-half years to complete. This would be followed by an additional year of testing, leading to an anticipated implementation in 2010.[54]

On August 23, 2007, TSA published a notice of proposed rulemaking (NPRM) for implementing Secure Flight, as well as an NPRM proposing Privacy Act exemptions for Secure Flight,[55] in the *Federal Register*. A Privacy Act System of Records Notice (SORN)[56] was also published in the same edition of the *Federal Register*. In addition, a Privacy Impact Assessment (PIA) for Secure Flight was posted on the TSA website.[57]

Along with the Secure Flight NPRM, on August 23, 2007, TSA published a related but separate final rule regarding the Advance Passenger Information System (APIS) administered by U.S. Customs and Border Protection (CBP) for screening passengers of international flights departing from or arriving to the United States.[58] TSA states

> We propose that, when the Secure Flight rule becomes final, aircraft operators would submit passenger information to DHS through a single DHS portal for both the Secure Flight and APIS programs. This would allow DHS to integrate the watch list matching component of APIS into Secure Flight, resulting in one DHS system responsible for watch list matching for all aviation passengers.[59]

According to the August 23, 2007 Secure Flight NPRM, in accordance with the Intelligence Reform and Terrorism Prevention Act (IRTPA), "TSA would receive passenger and certain non-traveler information, conduct watch list matching against the No Fly and Selectee portions of the Federal Government's consolidated terrorist watch list, and transmit boarding pass printing instructions back to aircraft operators."[60] Currently, air carriers are responsible for comparing passenger information to that on government watch lists.

The NPRM states that TSA would collect Secure Flight Passenger Data that includes a combination of required and optional information. Passengers would be required to provide their full names, "as it appears on a verifying identity document held by that individual."[61] In addition, passengers would be asked, but not required, to provide their date of birth, gender, Redress Number or known traveler number. However, the NPRM does propose circumstances in which aircraft operators would be required to provide the optional information to TSA if it already has obtained that information "in the ordinary course of business." The NPRM states

> If a covered aircraft operator were to input data required to be requested from individuals into the system where it stores SFPD — such as data from a passenger profile stored by the aircraft operator in the ordinary course of business — the aircraft operator would be required to include that data as part of the SFPD transmitted to TSA, even though the individual did not provide that information at the time of reservation.[62]

In addition, aircraft operations would be required to provide TSA, if available, a passenger's passport information, and "certain non-personally identifiable data fields" including itinerary information, reservation control number, record sequence number, record type, passenger update indicator, and traveler reference number.[63] Secure Flight would not utilize commercial data to verify identities, nor would it use algorithms to assign risk scores to individuals.[64]

In the NPRM TSA proposes a tiered data retention schedule. The purpose for retaining the records would be to facilitate a redress process, expedite future travel, and investigate and document terrorist events. Under this schedule, the records for "individuals not identified as potential matches by the automated matching tool would be retained for seven days" after the completion of directional travel. The records for individuals identified as "potential matches" would be retained for seven years following the completion of directional travel. The records of individuals identified as "confirmed matches" would be retained for 99 years.[65]

This original NPRM included a 60-day comment period, ending on October 22, 2007. However, in response to deadline extension requests received, on October 24, 2007, TSA published a notice in the Federal Register extending the public comment period an additional 30 days, ending November 21, 2007.[66]

On November 9, 2007, TSA published a final SORN[67] and a final rule regarding Privacy Act exemptions for Secure Flight.[68]

Multistate Anti-Terrorism Information Exchange (MATRIX) Pilot Project

Similar to TIA and CAPPS II, which were born out of an initial reaction to concerns about terrorism, the impetus and initial work on MATRIX grew out of the September 11, 2001 terrorist attacks. MATRIX was initially developed by Seisint, a Florida-based information products company, in an effort to facilitate collaborative information sharing and factual data analysis. At the outset of the project, MATRIX included a component Seisint called the High Terrorist Factor (HTF). Within days of the terrorist attacks, based on an analysis of information that included "age and gender, what they did with their drivers license, either pilots or associations to pilots, proximity to 'dirty' addresses/phone numbers, investigational data, how they shipped; how they received, social security number anomalies, credit history, and ethnicity," Seisint generated a list of 120,000 names with high HTF scores, or so-called terrorism quotients. Seisint provided this list to the Federal Bureau of Investigation (FBI), the Immigration and Naturalization Service (INS), the United States Secret Service (USSS), and the Florida Department of Law Enforcement (FDLE), which, according to a January 2003 presentation, made by the company, led to "several arrests within one week" and "scores of other arrests."[69] Although the HTF scoring system appeared to attract the interest of officials, this feature was reportedly dropped from MATRIX because it relied on intelligence data not normally available to the law enforcement community and concerns about privacy abuses. However, some critics of MATRIX continued to raise questions about HTF, citing the lack of any publicly available official documentation verifying such a decision.[70]

As a pilot project, MATRIX was administered through a collaborative effort between Seisint, the FDLE,[71] and the Institute for Intergovernmental Research (IIR), a "Florida-based nonprofit research and training organization, [that] specializes in law enforcement, juvenile justice, and criminal justice issues."[72] The Florida Department of Law Enforcement (FDLE) served as the "Security Agent" for MATRIX, administering control over which agencies and individuals had access to the system. FDLE was also a participant state in MATRIX. IIR was responsible for administrative support, and was the grantee for federal funds received for MATRIX.[73]

The analytical core of the MATRIX pilot project was an application called Factual Analysis Criminal Threat Solution (FACTS). FACTS was described as a "technological, investigative tool allowing query-based searches of available state and public records in the data reference repository."[74] The FACTS application allowed an authorized user to search "dynamically combined records from disparate datasets" based on partial information, and will "assemble" the results.[75] The data reference repository used with FACTS represented the amalgamation of over 3.9 billion public records collected from thousands of sources.[76] Some of the data contained in FACTS included FAA pilot licenses and aircraft ownership records, property ownership records, information on vessels registered with the Coast Guard, state sexual offenders lists, federal terrorist watch lists, corporation filings, Uniform Commercial Code filings, bankruptcy filings, state-issued professional licenses, criminal history information, department of corrections information and photo images, driver's license information and photo images, motor vehicle registration information, and information from commercial sources that "are generally available to the public or legally permissible under federal law."[77] The data reference repository purportedly excluded data such as telemarketing call lists, direct mail mailing lists, airline reservations or travel records, frequent flyer/hotel stay program membership or activity, magazine subscriptions, information about purchases made at retailers or over the Internet, telephone calling logs or records, credit or debit card numbers, mortgage or car payment information, bank account numbers or balance information, birth certificates, marriage licenses, divorce decrees, or utility bill payment information.

Participating law enforcement agencies utilized this information sharing and data mining resource over the Regional Information Sharing Systems (RISS) secure intranet (RISSNET). The RISS Program is an established system of six regional centers that are used to "share intelligence and coordinate efforts against criminal networks that operate in many locations across jurisdictional lines."[78] The RISS Program is used to combat traditional law enforcement targets, such as drug trafficking and violent crime, as well as other activities, such as terrorism and cybercrime. According to its website, RISS has been in operation for nearly 25 years, and has "member agencies in all 50 states, the District of Columbia, U.S. territories, Australia, Canada, and England."[79]

Some critics of MATRIX suggested that the original intentions and design of the pilot project echoed those of DARPA's highly criticized TIA program.[80] However, while it is difficult to ascribe intention, an ongoing series of problems did appear to have affected the trajectory of the project. In August 2003, Hank Asher, the founder of Seisint, resigned from the company's board of directors after questions about his criminal history were raised during contract negotiations between Seisint and the Florida Department of Law Enforcement. In the 1 980s, Asher was allegedly a pilot in several drug smuggling cases. However, he was reportedly never charged in the cases in exchange for his testimony at state and federal trials. Similar concerns had surfaced in 1999 when the FBI and the U.S. Drug Enforcement Agency (DEA) reportedly cancelled contracts with an earlier company Asher founded, DBT Online, Inc.[81]

Some civil liberties organizations also raised concerns about law enforcement actions being taken based on algorithms and analytical criteria developed by a private corporation, in this case Seisint, without any public or legislative input.[82] Questions also were raised about the level of involvement of the federal government, particularly the Department of Homeland Security and the Department of Justice, in a project that is ostensibly focused on supporting state-based information sharing.[83] It has been reported that the MATRIX pilot project has received a total of $12 million in federal funding — $8 million from the Office of Domestic

Preparedness (ODP) at the Department of Homeland Security (DHS), and $4 million from the Bureau of Justice Assistance (BJA) at the Department of Justice (DOJ).[84]

The MATRIX pilot project also suffered some setbacks in recruiting states to participate. The lack of participation can be especially troubling for a networked information sharing project such as MATRIX because, as Metcalfe's Law suggests, "the power of the network increases exponentially by the number of computers connected to it."[85] While as many as 16 states were reported to have either participated or seriously considered participating in MATRIX, several chose to withdraw, leaving a total of four states (Connecticut, Florida, Ohio, and Pennsylvania) at the conclusion of the pilot on April 15, 2005. State officials cited a variety of reasons for not participating in MATRIX, including costs, concerns about violating state privacy laws, and duplication of existing resources.[86]

In its news release announcing the conclusion of the pilot, the FDLE stated that as a proof-of-concept pilot study from July 2003 to April 2005, MATRIX had achieved many "operational successes." Among the statistics cited, the news release stated that

- Between July 2003 and April 2005, there have been 1,866,202 queries to the FACTS application.
- As of April 8, 2005, there were 963 law enforcement users accessing FACTS.
- FACTS assisted a variety of investigations. On average, cases pertained to the following:

  - Fraud — 22.6%
  - Robbery — 18.8%
  - Sex Crime Investigations — 8.6%
  - Larceny and Theft — 8.3%
  - Extortion/Blackmail — 7.0%
  - Burglary/Breaking and Entering — 6.8%
  - Stolen Property — 6.2%
  - Terrorism/National Security — 2.6%
  - Other — 19.1% (e.g., assault, arson, narcotics, homicide)

It was also announced that while the pilot study would not be continued, due to a lack of additional federal funding, that Florida and other participating states were "independently negotiating the continued use of the FACTS application for use within their individual state[s]."[87]

Other Data Mining Initiatives

Able Danger

In summer 2005, news reports began to appear regarding a data mining initiative that had been carried out by the U.S. Army's Land Information Warfare Agency (LIWA) in 1999-2000. The initiative, referred to as Able Danger, had reportedly been requested by the U.S. Special Operations Command (SOCOM) as part of larger effort to develop a plan to combat transnational terrorism. Because the details of Able Danger remain classified, little is known about the program. However, in a briefing to reporters, the Department of Defense characterized Able Danger as a demonstration project to test analytical methods and technology on very large amounts of data.[88] The project involved using link analysis to identify underlying connections and associations between individuals who otherwise appear to have no outward connection with one another. The link analysis used both classified and open source data, totaling a reported 2.5 terabytes.[89] All of this data, which included information on U.S. persons, was reportedly deleted in April 2000 due to U.S. Army regulations requiring information on U.S. persons be destroyed after a project ends or becomes inactive.[90]

Interest in Able Danger was largely driven by controversy over allegations that the data mining analysis had resulted in the identification of Mohammed Atta, one of the 9/11 hijackers, as a terrorist suspect before the attacks took place. While some individuals who had been involved in Able Danger were reportedly prepared to testify that they had seen either his name and/or picture on a chart prior to the attacks, the identification claim was strongly disputed by others.

On September 21, 2005, the Senate Committee on the Judiciary held a hearing on Able Danger to consider how the data could or should have been shared with other agencies, and whether the destruction of the data was in fact required by the relevant regulations. While the Department of Defense directed the individuals involved in Able Danger not to testify at the hearing, testimony was taken from the attorney of one of the individuals, as well as others not directly involved with the project.

On February 15, 2006, the House Committee on Armed Services Subcommittee on Strategic Forces and Subcommittee on Terrorism, Unconventional Threats and Capabilities held a joint hearing on Able Danger. The first half of the hearing was held in open session while the second half of the hearing was held in closed session to allow for the discussion of classified information. Witnesses testifying during the open session included Stephen Cambone, Undersecretary of Defense for Intelligence; Erik Kleinsmith; Anthony Shaffer, and J.D. Smith.

In September 2006, a Department of Defense Inspector General report regarding Able Danger was released. The investigation examined allegations of mismanagement of the Able Danger program and reprisals against Lieutenant Colonel (LTC) Anthony Shaffer, a member of the U.S. Army Reserve and civilian employee of the Defense Intelligence Agency (DIA). The DoD Inspector General "found some procedural oversights concerning the DIA handling of LTC Shaffer's office contents and his Officer Evaluation Reports." However, the investigation found that

> The evidence did not support assertions that Able Danger identified the September 11, 2001, terrorists nearly a year before the attack, that Able Danger team members were prohibited from sharing information with law enforcement authorities, or that DoD officials reprised against LTC Shaffer for his disclosures regarding Able Danger.[91]

In December 2006, the then-Chairman and then-Vice Chairman of the Senate Select Committee on Intelligence, Senator Roberts and Senator Rockefeller respectively, released a letter summarizing the findings of a review of Able Danger conducted by Committee staff.[92] According to the letter, the results of the review, begun in August 2005, "were confirmed in all respects by the DoD Inspector General investigation of the Able Danger program (Case Number H05L979052 1)." The letter further stated that the review "revealed no evidence to support the underlying Able Danger allegations" and that the Committee considered the matter "closed."

Automated Targeting System (ATS)

On November 2, 2006, DHS posted a System of Records Notice (SORN) in the Federal Register regarding the deployment of the Automated Targeting System (ATS), to screen travelers entering the United States by car, plane, ship, or rail.[93] Originally developed to help identify potential cargo threats, ATS is a module of the Treasure Enforcement Communications System (TECS). TECS is described as an "overarching law enforcement information collection, targeting, and sharing environment." ATS is run by the Bureau of Customs and Border Protection (CPB). The Federal Register notice states that "ATS builds a risk assessment for cargo, conveyances, and travelers based on criteria and rules developed by CPB." The notice further states that "ATS both collects information directly, and derives other information from various systems." Information collected may be retained for up to forty years "to cover the potentially active lifespan of individuals associated with terrorism or other criminal activities."

According to a November 22, 2006 privacy impact assessment, ATS itself is composed of six modules:

- AT S-Inbound — inbound cargo and conveyances (rail, truck, ship, and air)
- AT S-Outbound — outbound cargo and conveyances (rail, truck, ship, and air)
- ATS-Passenger (ATS-P) — travelers and conveyances (air, ship, and rail)
- AT S-Land (ATS-L) — private vehicles arriving by land
- ATS-International (ATS-I) — cargo targeting for CPB's collaboration with foreign customs authorities
- ATS-Trend Analysis and Analytical Selectivity Program (ATS-TAP) (analytical module)[94]

According to DHS, "ATS historically was covered by the SORN for TECS." The November 2, 2006 SORN was "solely to provide increased noticed and transparency to the public about ATS" and "did not describe any new collection of information."[95] However, the disclosure raised a number of issues about various facets of the program, including proposed exemptions from the Privacy Act; opportunities for citizens to correct errors in the records; how the risk assessments are created; if any previous testing has been conducted; and the effectiveness of the system.

In its July 6, 2007 report to Congress, the DHS Privacy Office stated that of the six modules that compose ATS, only two — ATS Inbound and ATS Outbound (which became operational in 1997) — "engage in data mining to provide decision support analysis for targeting of cargo for suspicious activity."[96] In contrast, the DHS Privacy Office report states that the ATS Passenger module does not meet the definition of data mining referred to in H.Rept. 109-699 (this definition is discussed in more detail in "Legislation in the 109th Congress," below). Whereas the ATS Passenger module calls for a search or examination of a traveler based on the traveler's personally identifying travel documents, the data mining definition in H.Rept. 109-699 only includes a search that "does not use a specific individual's personal identifiers to acquire information concerning that individual."[97]

On August 6, 2007, the Privacy Office of the Department of Homeland Security published a notice of proposed rulemaking (NPRM) proposing Privacy Act exemptions for the Automated Targeting System,[98] in the *Federal Register*. A Privacy Act System of Records Notice (SORN)[99] was also published in the same edition of the *Federal Register*. In addition, a revised Privacy Impact Assessment (PIA) for ATS was posted on the DHS website.[100]

According to the NPRM, AT S-P module records exempt from the Privacy Act would include "the risk assessment analyses and business confidential information received in the PNR from the air and vessel carriers." Records or information obtained from other systems of records that are exempt from certain provisions of the Privacy Act would retain their exemption in AT S.[101] In the NPRM, DHS states that the exemptions are needed "to protect information relating to law enforcement investigations from disclosures to subjects of investigations and others who could interfere with investigatory and law enforcement activities."

The August 6, 2007 SORN is a revised version of the November 2, 2006 SORN "which responds to those comments [received in response to the November 2006 SORN], makes certain amendments with regard to the retention period and access provisions of the prior notice, and provides further notice and transparency to the public about the functionality of ATS."[102] The changes include

- Reducing the "general retention period for data maintained in ATS" from 40 to 15 years, and adding a requirement that users obtain supervisory approval to access archived data in the last eight years of the retention period.
- Allowing "persons whose PNR data has been collected and maintained in AT S-P [to] have administrative access to that data under the Privacy Act." Individuals will also be able to "seek to correct factual inaccuracies contained in their PNR data, as it is maintained by CBP."
- Adding book agents as a category of people from whom information is obtained, in acknowledgment that book agents' identities are included in itinerary information.
- Amending the categories of people covered by ATS "to include persons who international itineraries cause their flight to stop in the United States, either to refuel or permit a transfer, and crewmembers on flights that overly or transit through U.S. airspace."
- Clarifying "the categories of PNR data collected and maintained in ATS-P to more accurately reflect the type of data collected from air carriers."
- Removing "two of the routine uses included in the earlier version of the SORN — those pertaining to using ATS in background checks."

This revised SORN became effective on September 5, 2007.

National Security Agency (NSA) and the Terrorist Surveillance Program

In December 2005 news reports appeared for the first time revealing the existence of a classified NSA terrorist surveillance program, dating back to at least 2002, involving the domestic collection, analysis, and sharing of telephone call information.[103] Controversy over the program raised congressional concerns about both the prevalence of homeland security data mining and the capacity of the country's intelligence and law enforcement agencies to adequately analyze and share counterterrorism information. The Senate Committee on the Judiciary held two hearings regarding the issue on February 6 and February 28, 2006.

Although details about the program are classified, statements by President Bush and Administration officials following the initial revelation of the program suggested that the NSA terrorist surveillance program focused only on international calls, with a specific goal of targeting the communications of al Qaeda and related terrorist groups, and affiliated individuals. It was also suggested that the program was reviewed and reauthorized on a regular basis and that key Members of Congress had been briefed about the program.

In his weekly radio address on December 17, 2005, President Bush stated:

> In the weeks following the terrorist attacks on our nation, I authorized the National Security Agency, consistent with U.S. law and the Constitution, to intercept the international communications of people with known links to al Qaeda and related terrorist organizations. Before we intercept these communications, the government must have information that establishes a clear link to these terrorist networks.[104]

President Bush also stated during his radio address:

The activities I authorized are reviewed approximately every 45 days. Each review is based on a fresh intelligence assessment of terrorist threats to the continuity of our government and the threat of catastrophic damage to our homeland. During each assessment, previous activities under the authorization are reviewed. The review includes approval by our nation's top legal officials, including the Attorney General and the Counsel to the President. I have reauthorized this program more than 30 times since the September the 11th attacks, and I intend to do so for as long as our nation faces a continuing threat from al Qaeda and related groups.[105]

In a January 27, 2006, public release statement, the Department of Justice stated:

> The NSA program is narrowly focused, aimed only at international calls and targeted at al Qaeda and related groups. Safeguards are in place to protect the civil liberties of ordinary Americans.
>
> - The program only applies to communications where one party is located outside of the United States.
> - The NSA terrorist surveillance program described by the President is only focused on members of Al Qaeda and affiliated groups. Communications are only intercepted if there is a reasonable basis to believe that one party to the communication is a member of al Qaeda, affiliated with al Qaeda, or a member of an organization affiliated with al Qaeda.
> - The program is designed to target a key tactic of al Qaeda: infiltrating foreign agents into the United States and controlling their movements through electronic communications, just as it did leading up to the September 11 attacks.
> - The NSA activities are reviewed and reauthorized approximately every 45 days. In addition, the General Counsel and Inspector General of the NSA monitor the program to ensure that it is operating properly and that civil liberties are protected, and the intelligence agents involved receive extensive training.[106]

On February 6, 2006, in his written statement for a Senate Committee on the Judiciary hearing, U.S. Attorney General Gonzalez stated:

> The terrorist surveillance program targets communications where one party to the communication is outside the U.S. and the government has "reasonable grounds to believe" that at least one party to the communication is a member or agent of al Qaeda, or an affiliated terrorist organization. This program is reviewed and reauthorized by the President approximately every 45 days. The Congressional leadership, including the leaders of the Intelligence Committees of both Houses of Congress, has been briefed about this program more than a dozen times since 2001. The program provides the United States with the early warning system we so desperately needed on September 10th.[107]

In May 2006 news reports alleged additional details regarding the NSA terrorist surveillance program, renewing concerns about the possible existence of inappropriately authorized domestic surveillance. According to these reports, following the September 11, 2001 attacks, the NSA contracted with AT&T, Verizon, and BellSouth to collect information about domestic telephone calls handled by these companies. The NSA, in turn, reportedly used this information to conduct "social network analysis" to map relationships between people based on their communications.[108]

It remains unclear precisely what information, if any, was collected and provided to the NSA. Some reports suggest that personally identifiable information (i.e., names, addresses, etc.) were not included. It also has been reported that the content of the calls (what was spoken) was not collected. Since the emergence of these news reports, BellSouth has issued a public statement saying that according to an internal review conducted by the company, "no such [alleged] contract exists" and that the company has "not provided bulk customer calling records to the NSA."[109] Similarly, Verizon has issued a public statement saying that due to the classified nature of the NSA program, "Verizon cannot and will not confirm or deny whether it has any relationship to the classified NSA program," but that "Verizon's wireless and wireline companies did not provide to NSA customer records or call data, local or otherwise."[110] Together, AT&T, Verizon, and BellSouth are the three largest telecommunications companies in the United States, serving more than 200 million customers, accounting for hundreds of billions of calls each year.[111]

In a January 17, 2007 letter to the Senate Committee on the Judiciary, then-Attorney General Gonzalez wrote that:

> a Judge of the Foreign Intelligence Surveillance Court issued orders authorizing the Government to target for collection international communications into or out of the United States where there is probable cause to believe that one of the communicants is a member or agent of al Qaeda or an associated terrorist organization. As a result of these orders, any electronic surveillance that was occurring as part of the Terrorist Surveillance Program will now be conducted subject to the approval of the Foreign Intelligence Surveillance Court.[112]

The letter further stated that "the President has determined not to reauthorize the Terrorist Surveillance Program when the current authorization expires."

The program and the alleged involvement of telecommunications companies continues to be the subject of several lawsuits. For a discussion of these legal issues, see CRS Report RL3 3424, *Government Access to Phone Calling Activity and Related Records: Legal Authorities*, by Elizabeth B. Bazan, Gina Marie Stevens, and Brian T. Yeh. Congress is also considering an option to provide a measure of retroactive immunity to telecommunications companies that participated in government counterterrorism surveillance activities between September 11, 2001, and January 17, 2007, as a provision of S. 2248, the Foreign Intelligence Surveillance Act of 1978

Amendments Act of 2007. For a discussion of this legislation, see CRS Report RL33539, *Intelligence Issues for Congress*, by Richard A. Best, Jr.

Novel Intelligence from Massive Data (NIDM) Program

As part of its efforts to better utilize the overwhelming flow of information it collects, NSA has reportedly been supporting the development of new technology and data management techniques by funding grants given by the Advanced Research Development Activity (ARDA). ARDA is an intelligence community (IC) organization whose mission is described as "to sponsor high-risk, high-payoff research designed to leverage leading edge technology to solve some of the most critical problems facing the Intelligence Community (IC)."[113] ARDA's research support is organized into various technology "thrusts" representing the most critical areas of development. Some of ARDA's research thrusts include Information Exploitation, Quantum Information Science, Global Infosystems Access, Novel Intelligence from Massive Data, and Advanced Information Assurance.

The Novel Intelligence from Massive Data (NIMD) program focuses on the development of data mining and analysis tools to be used in working with massive data.[114] Novel intelligence refers to "actionable information not previously known." Massive data refers to data that has characteristics that are especially challenging to common data analysis tools and methods. These characteristics can include unusual volume, breadth (heterogeneity), and complexity. Data sets that are one petabyte (one quadrillion bytes) or larger are considered to be "massive." Smaller data sets that contain items in a wide variety of formats, or are very heterogeneous (i.e., unstructured text, spoken text, audio, video, graphs, diagrams, images, maps, equations, chemical formulas, tables, etc.) can also be considered "massive." According to ARDA's website (no longer available)[115] "some intelligence data sources grow at a rate of four petabytes per month now, and the rate of growth is increasing." With the continued proliferation of both the means and volume of electronic communications, it is expected that the need for more sophisticated tools will intensify. Whereas some observers once predicted that the NSA was in danger of becoming proverbially deaf due to the spreading use of encrypted communications, it appears that NSA may now be at greater risk of being "drowned" in information.

DATA MINING ISSUES

As data mining initiatives continue to evolve, there are several issues Congress may decide to consider related to implementation and oversight. These issues include, but are not limited to, data quality, interoperability, mission creep, and privacy. As with other aspects of data mining, while technological capabilities are important, other factors also influence the success of a project's outcome.

Data Quality

Data quality is a multifaceted issue that represents one of the biggest challenges for data mining. Data quality refers to the accuracy and completeness of the data. Data quality can also be affected by the structure and consistency of the data being analyzed. The presence of duplicate records, the lack of data standards, the timeliness of updates, and human error can significantly impact the effectiveness of the more complex data mining techniques, which are sensitive to subtle differences that may exist in the data. To improve data quality, it is sometimes necessary to "clean" the data, which can involve the removal of duplicate records, normalizing the values used to represent information in the database (e.g., ensuring that "no" is represented as a 0 throughout the database, and not sometimes as a 0, sometimes as an N, etc.), accounting for missing data points, removing unneeded data fields, identifying anomalous data points (e.g., an individual whose age is shown as 142 years), and standardizing data formats (e.g., changing dates so they all include MM/DD/YYYY).

Interoperability

Related to data quality, is the issue of interoperability of different databases and data mining software. Interoperability refers to the ability of a computer system and/or data to work with other systems or data using common standards or processes. Interoperability is a critical part of the larger efforts to improve interagency collaboration and information sharing through e-government and homeland security initiatives. For data mining, interoperability of databases and software is important to enable the search and analysis of multiple databases simultaneously, and to help ensure the compatibility of data mining activities of different agencies. Data mining projects that are trying to take advantage of existing legacy databases or that are initiating first-time collaborative efforts with other agencies or levels of government (e.g., police departments in different states) may experience interoperability problems. Similarly, as agencies move forward with the creation of new databases and information sharing efforts, they will need to address interoperability issues during their planning stages to better ensure the effectiveness of their data mining projects.

Mission Creep

Mission creep is one of the leading risks of data mining cited by civil libertarians, and represents how control over one's information can be a tenuous proposition. Mission creep refers to the use of data for purposes other than that for which the data was originally collected. This can occur regardless of whether the data was provided voluntarily by the individual or was collected through other means.

Efforts to fight terrorism can, at times, take on an acute sense of urgency. This urgency can create pressure on both data holders and officials who access the data. To leave an available resource unused may appear to some as being negligent. Data holders may feel obligated to make any information available that could be used to prevent a future attack or track a known terrorist. Similarly, government officials responsible for ensuring the safety of others may be pressured to use and/or combine existing databases to identify potential threats. Unlike physical searches, or the detention of individuals, accessing information for purposes other than originally intended may appear to be a victimless or harmless exercise. However, such information use can lead to unintended outcomes and produce misleading results.

One of the primary reasons for misleading results is inaccurate data. All data collection efforts suffer accuracy concerns to some degree. Ensuring the accuracy of information can require costly protocols that may not be cost effective if the data is not of inherently high economic value. In well-managed data mining projects, the original data collecting organization is likely to be aware of the data's limitations and account for these limitations accordingly. However, such awareness may not be communicated or heeded when data is used for other purposes. For example, the accuracy of information collected through a shopper's club card may suffer for a variety of reasons, including the lack of identity authentication when a card is issued, cashiers using their own cards for customers who do not have one, and/or customers who use multiple cards.[116] For the purposes of marketing to consumers, the impact of these inaccuracies is negligible to the individual. If a government agency were to use that information to target individuals based on food purchases associated with particular religious observances though, an outcome based on inaccurate information could be, at the least, a waste of resources by the government agency, and an unpleasant experience for the misidentified individual. As the March 2004 TAPAC report observes, the potential wide reuse of data suggests that concerns about mission creep can extend beyond privacy to the protection of civil rights in the event that information is used for "targeting an individual solely on the basis of religion or expression, or using information in a way that would violate the constitutional guarantee against self-incrimination."[117]

Privacy

As additional information sharing and data mining initiatives have been announced, increased attention has focused on the implications for privacy. Concerns about privacy focus both on actual projects proposed, as well as concerns about the potential for data mining applications to be expanded beyond their original purposes (mission creep). For example, some experts suggest that anti-terrorism data mining applications might also be useful for combating other types of crime as well.[118] So far there has been little consensus about how data mining should be carried out, with several competing points of view being debated. Some observers contend that tradeoffs may need to be made regarding privacy to ensure security. Other observers suggest that existing laws and regulations regarding privacy protections are adequate, and that these initiatives do not pose any threats to privacy.

Still other observers argue that not enough is known about how data mining projects will be carried out, and that greater oversight is needed. There is also some disagreement over how privacy concerns should be addressed. Some observers suggest that technical solutions are adequate. In contrast, some privacy advocates argue in favor of creating clearer policies and exercising stronger oversight. As data mining efforts move forward, Congress may consider a variety of questions including, the degree to which government agencies should use and mix commercial data with government data, whether data sources are being used for purposes other than those for which they were originally designed, and the possible application of the Privacy Act to these initiatives.

Legislation in the 108th Congress

During the 108th Congress, a number of legislative proposals were introduced that would restrict data mining activities by some parts of the federal government, and/or increase the reporting requirements of such projects to Congress. For example, on January 16, 2003, Senator Feingold introduced S. 188 the Data-Mining Moratorium Act of 2003, which would have imposed a moratorium on the implementation of data mining under the Total Information Awareness program (now referred to as the Terrorism Information Awareness project) by the Department of Defense, as well as any similar program by the Department of Homeland Security.

S. 188 was referred to the Committee on the Judiciary.

On January 23, 2003, Senator Wyden introduced S.Amdt. 59, an amendment to H.J.Res. 2, the Omnibus Appropriations Act for Fiscal Year 2003. As passed in its final form as part of the omnibus spending bill (P.L. 108-7) on February 13, 2003, and signed by the President on February 20, 2003, the amendment requires the Director of Central Intelligence, the Secretary of Defense, and the Attorney General to submit a joint report to Congress within 90 days providing details about the TIA program.[119] Some of the information required includes spending schedules, likely effectiveness of the program, likely impact on privacy and civil liberties, and any laws and regulations that may need to be changed to fully deploy TIA. If the report was not submitted within 90 days, funding for the TIA program could have been discontinued.[120] Funding for TIA was later discontinued in Section 8131 of the FY2004 Department of Defense Appropriations Act (P.L. 108-87), signed into law on September 30, 2003.[121]

On March 13, 2003, Senator Wyden introduced an amendment to S. 165, the Air Cargo Security Act, requiring the Secretary of Homeland Security to submit a report to Congress within 90 days providing information about the impact of CAPPS II on privacy and civil liberties. The amendment was passed by the Committee on Commerce, Science, and Transportation, and the bill was forwarded for consideration by the full Senate (S.Rept. 108-38). In May 2003, S. 165 was passed by the Senate with the Wyden amendment included and was sent to the House where it was referred to the Committee on Transportation and Infrastructure.

Funding restrictions on CAPPS II were included in section 519 of the FY2004 Department of Homeland Security Appropriations Act (P.L. 108-90), signed into law October 1, 2003. This provision included restrictions on the "deployment or implementation, on other than a test basis, of the Computer-Assisted Passenger Prescreening System (CAPP SII)," pending the completion of a GAO report regarding the efficacy, accuracy, and security of CAPPS II, as well as the existence of a system of an appeals process for individuals identified as a potential threat by the system.[122] In its report delivered to Congress in February 2004, GAO reported that "As of January 1, 2004, TSA has not fully addressed seven of the eight CAPPS II issues identified by the Congress as key areas of interest."[123] The one issue GAO determined that TSA had addressed is the establishment of an internal oversight board. GAO attributed the incomplete progress on these issues partly to the "early stage of the system's development."[124]

On March 25, 2003, the House Committee on Government Reform Subcommittee on Technology, Information Policy, Intergovernmental Relations, and the Census held a hearing on the current and future possibilities of data mining. The witnesses, drawn from federal and state government, industry, and academia, highlighted a number of perceived strengths and weaknesses of data mining, as well as the still-evolving nature of the technology and practices behind data mining.[125] While data mining was alternatively described by some witnesses as a process, and by other witnesses as a productivity tool, there appeared to be a general consensus that the challenges facing the future development and success of government data mining applications were related less to technological concerns than to other issues such as data integrity, security, and privacy. On May 6 and May 20, 2003 the Subcommittee also held hearings on the potential opportunities and challenges for using factual data analysis for national security purposes.

On July 29, 2003, Senator Wyden introduced S. 1484, The Citizens' Protection in Federal Databases Act, which was referred to the Committee on the Judiciary. Among its provisions, S. 1484 would have required the Attorney General, the Secretary of Defense, the Secretary of Homeland Security, the Secretary of the Treasury, the Director of Central Intelligence, and the Director of the Federal Bureau of Investigation to submit to Congress a report containing information regarding the purposes, type of data, costs, contract durations, research methodologies, and other details before obligating or spending any funds on commercially available databases. S. 1484 would also have set restrictions on the conduct of searches or analysis of databases "based solely on a hypothetical scenario or hypothetical supposition of who may commit a crime or pose a threat to national security."

On July 31, 2003, Senator Feingold introduced S. 1544, the Data-Mining Reporting Act of 2003, which was referred to the Committee on the Judiciary. Among its provisions, S. 1544 would have required any department or agency engaged in data mining to submit a public report to Congress regarding these activities. These reports would have been required to include a variety of details about the data mining project, including a description of the technology and data to be used, a discussion of how the technology will be used and when it will be deployed, an assessment of the expected efficacy of the data mining project, a privacy impact assessment, an analysis of the relevant laws and regulations that would govern the project, and a discussion of procedures for informing individuals their personal information will be used and allowing them to opt out, or an explanation of why such procedures are not in place.

Also on July 31, 2003, Senator Murkowski introduced S. 1552, the Protecting the Rights of Individuals Act, which was referred to the Committee on the Judiciary. Among its provisions, section 7 of S. 1552 would have imposed a moratorium on data mining by any federal department or agency "except pursuant to a law specifically authorizing such data-mining program or activity by such department or agency." It also would have required

> The head of each department or agency of the Federal Government that engages or plans to engage in any activities relating to the development or use of a data- mining program or activity shall submit to Congress, and make available to the public, a report on such activities.

On May 5, 2004, Representative McDermott introduced H.R. 4290, the Data- Mining Reporting Act of 2004, which was referred to the House Committee on Government Reform Subcommittee on Technology, Information Policy, Intergovernmental Relations, and the Census. H.R. 4290 would have required

> each department or agency of the Federal Government that is engaged in any activity or use or develop data-mining technology shall each submit a public report to Congress on all such activities of the department or agency under the jurisdiction of that official.

A similar provision was included in H.R. 4591/S. 2528, the Civil Liberties Restoration Act of 2004. S. 2528 was introduced by Senator Kennedy on June 16, 2004 and referred to the Committee on the Judiciary. H.R. 4591 was introduced by Representative Berman on June 16, 2004 and referred to the Committee on the Judiciary and the Permanent Select Committee on Intelligence.

Legislation in the 109TH Congress

Data mining continued to be a subject of interest to Congress in the 109th Congress. On April 6, 2005, H.R. 1502, the Civil Liberties Restoration Act of 2005 was introduced by Representative Berman and was referred to the Committee on the Judiciary[126], the Permanent Select Committee on Intelligence, and the Committee on Homeland Security. Section 402, Data-Mining Report, of H.R. 1502 would have required that

> The Head of each department or agency of the Federal Government that is engaged in any activity or use or develop data-mining technology shall each submit a public report to Congress on all such activities of the department or agency under the jurisdiction of that official.

As part of their content, these reports would have been required to provide, for each data mining activity covered by H.R. 1502, information regarding the technology and data being used; information on how the technology would be used and the target dates for deployment; an assessment of the likely efficacy of the data mining technology; an assessment of the likely impact of the activity on privacy and civil liberties; a list and analysis of the laws and regulations that would apply to the data mining activity and whether these laws and regulations would need to be modified to allow the data mining activity to be implemented; information on the policies, procedures, and guidelines that would be developed and applied to protect the privacy and due process rights of individuals, and ensure that only accurate information is collected and used; and information on how individuals whose information is being used in the data mining activity will be notified of the use of their information, and, if applicable, what options will be available for individual to opt-out of the activity. These reports would have been due to Congress no later than 90 days after the enactment of H.R. 1502, and would have been required to be updated annually to include "any new data-mining technologies."

On June 6, 2005, S. 1169, the Federal Agency Data-Mining Reporting Act of 2005 was introduced by Senator Feingold, and was referred to the Senate Committee on the Judiciary. Among its provisions, S. 1169 would have required any department or agency engaged in data mining to submit a public report to Congress regarding these activities. These reports would have been required to include a variety of details about the data mining project, including a description of the technology and data to be used, a discussion of the plans and goals for using the technology when it will be deployed, an assessment of the expected efficacy of the data mining project, a privacy impact assessment, an analysis of the relevant laws and regulations that would govern the project, and a discussion of procedures for informing individuals their personal information will be used and allowing them to opt out, or an explanation of why such procedures are not in place.

On July 11, 2005, H.R. 3199, the USA PATRIOT Improvement and Reauthorization Act of 2005 was introduced. On July 21, 2005, Representative Berman introduced H.Amdt. 497 to H.R. 3199, which would required the Attorney General to submit a report to Congress on the data mining initiatives of the Department of Justice and other departments and agencies as well. The provision stated, in part;

> The Attorney General shall collect the information described in paragraph (2) from the head of each department or agency of the Federal

> Government that is engaged in any activity to use or develop data-mining technology and shall report to Congress on all such activities.

H.Amdt. 497 was passed on July 21, 2005 by a 261-165 recorded vote and appeared as Section 132 of H.R. 3199. Also on this day, H.R. 3199 was passed by the House and sent to the Senate. On July 29, 2005, the Senate passed an amended version of H.R. 3199. The Senate version did not contain a comparable provision on data mining. The bill went to a House-Senate conference in November 2005. Section 126 of the conference report (H.Rept. 109-333) filed on December 8, 2005 included a provision for a report on data mining by the Department of Justice alone, rather than other departments and agencies as well. The provision stated, in part:

> Not later than one year after the date of enactment of this Act, the Attorney General shall submit to Congress a report on any initiative of the Department of Justice that uses or is intended to develop pattern-based data mining technology...

The bill was signed into law as P.L. 109-177 on March 9, 2006.

On October 6, 2005, H.R. 4009, the Department of Homeland Security Reform Act of 2005, was introduced by Representative Thompson, and was referred to the Committee on Homeland Security, the Permanent Select Committee on Intelligence, and the Committee on Transportation and Infrastructure. Section 203(c)(16) would have directed the Chief Intelligence Officer, as established in Section 203(a):

> To establish and utilize, in conjunction with the Chief Information Officer of the Department, a secure communications and information technology infrastructure, including data-mining and other advanced analytical tools, in order to access, receive, and analyze data and information in furtherance of the responsibilities under this section, and to disseminate information acquired and analyzed by the Department, as appropriate.

On December 6, 2005, H.R. 4437, the Border Protection, Antiterrorism, and Illegal Immigration Control Act of 2005 was introduced by Representative Sensenbrenner and was referred to the Committee on the Judiciary and the Committee on Homeland Security. On December 8, 2005, the Committee on the Judiciary held a markup session and ordered an amended version of H.R. 4437 to be reported. On December 13, 2005, the Committee on Homeland Security discharged the bill, which was subsequently referred to and discharged from the Committee on Education and the Workforce and the Committee on Ways and Means. On December 16, 2005, H.R. 4437 was passed by the House and sent to the Senate, where it was referred to the Committee on the Judiciary.

Section 1305, Authority of the Office of Security and Investigations to Detect and Investigate Immigration Benefits Fraud, of H.R. 4437 would have granted the Office of Security and Investigations of the United States Citizenship and Immigration Services at the Department of Homeland Security the authority to:

1 to conduct fraud detection operations, including data mining and analysis;
2 to investigate any criminal or noncriminal allegations of violations of the Immigration and Nationality Act or title 18, United States Code, that Immigration and Customs Enforcement declines to investigate;
3 to turn over to a United States Attorney for prosecution evidence that tends to establish such violations; and
4 to engage in information sharing, partnerships, and other collaborative efforts with any —

a Federal, State, or local law enforcement entity;
b foreign partners; or
c entity within the intelligence community (as defined in section 3(4) of the National Security Act of 1947 (50 U.S.C. 401a(4)).

On July 12, 2006, Senator Feingold introduced S.Amdt 4562 to H.R. 5441, the Homeland Security Department FY2007 appropriations bill. S.Amdt. 4562 is substantively similar to S. 1169, although only applies to departments and agencies within the Department of Homeland Security, rather than the entire federal government. S.Amdt. 4562 was agreed to by unanimous consent and was included in the Senate-passed version of H.R. 5441 as Section 549. According to the conference report (H.Rept. 109-699) Section 549 was deleted from the final bill that was passed into law (P.L. 109-295).[127] However, the conference report also included a statement on data mining by the conference managers expressing concern about the development and use of data mining technology and;

> "direct[s] the DHS Privacy Officer to submit a report consistent with the terms and conditions listed in section 549 of the Senate bill. The conferees expect the report to include information on how it has implemented the recommendation laid out in the Department's data mining report received July 18, 2006."[128]

LEGISLATION AND HEARINGS IN THE 110TH CONGRESS

Data mining has been the subject of some of the earliest proposed bills and hearings of the 1 10th Congress. On January 10, 2007, S. 236, the Federal Agency Data-Mining Reporting Act of 2007 was introduced by Senator Feingold and Senator Sununu, and was referred to the Senate Committee on the Judiciary. Among its provisions, S. 236 would require any department or agency engaged in data mining to submit a public report to Congress regarding these activities. These reports would be required to include a variety of details about the data mining project, including a description of the technology and data to be used, a discussion of the plans and goals for using the technology when it will be deployed, an assessment of the expected efficacy of the data mining project, a privacy impact assessment, an analysis of the relevant laws and regulations that would govern the project, and a discussion of procedures for informing individuals their personal information will be used and allowing them to opt out, or an explanation of why such procedures are not in place. [129]

Also in the Senate, the Committee on the Judiciary held a hearing on January 10, 2007 entitled "Balancing Privacy and Security: The Privacy Implications of Government Data Mining Programs." The witnesses included a former Member of Congress and several individuals from research centers and think tanks. Collectively, they highlighted a number of perceived strengths and weaknesses of data mining, as well as the continually evolving nature of the technology and practices behind data mining.[130] The witnesses also addressed the inherent challenge of simultaneously protecting the nation from terrorism while also protecting civil liberties.

On February 28, 2007, Senator Reid introduced S.Amdt. 275 to S. 4 the Improving America's Security by Implementing Unfinished Recommendations of the 9/11 Commission Act of 2007. Section 504 of this amendment, entitled the Federal Agency Data Mining Report Act of 2007, was identical to S. 236, as introduced. During the Senate floor debates held on S. 4 in early March 2007, several amendments to the data mining section of S. 4 were introduced.

On March 6, 2007, Senator Kyl introduced S.Amdt. 357 to S.Amdt. 275 of S. 4. The purpose of S.Amdt. 357 was described as "to amend the data-mining reporting requirement to protect existing patents, trade secrets, and confidential business processes, and to adopt a narrower definition of data mining in order to exclude routine computer searches."[131] Later on March 6, 2007, Senator Kyl offered a modification to S.Amdt. 357 that used definitions of data mining and database very similar to those that appear in P.L. 109-177 the USA PATRIOT Improvement and Reauthorization Act of 2005, and that slightly changed the original language of

S.Amdt. 357 regarding protection of patents and other proprietary business information.

On March 8, 2007, Senator Feingold introduced S.Amdt. 429 to S.Amdt. 275. S.Amdt. 429 is very similar to S. 236, as introduced, with a few differences. One difference is that the initial description used to partially define data mining is changed to include "a program involving pattern-based queries, searches, or other analyses of 1 or more electronic databases...." Another difference is that the data mining reporting requirement excludes data mining initiatives that are solely for "the detection of fraud, waste, or abuse in a Government agency or program; or the security of a Government computer system."[132] Another difference is the inclusion of language requiring that the data mining reports be "produced in coordination with the privacy officer of that department or agency."[133] S.Amdt. 429 also includes language detailing the types of information that should be included in the classified annexes of the data mining reports (i.e., classified information, law enforcement sensitive information, proprietary business information, and trade secrets), and states that such classified annexes should not be made available to the public.

Later on March 8, 2007, Senator Feingold introduced S.Amdt. 441 to S.Amdt. 357. S.Amdt. 441 is substantively the same as S.Amdt. 429, but with a technical modification.

On March 13, 2007, S.Amdt. 441 was agreed to by unanimous consent, and S.Amdt. 357, as modified, and as amended by S.Amdt. 441 was agreed to by unanimous consent. Also on March 13, 2007, S. 4 passed the Senate by a 60-38 vote. The data mining provision appears as Section 604 in S. 4. As originally passed by the House in January 2007, the House version of S. 4, H.R. 1, did not contain a comparable provision on data mining.

On March 21, 2007, the House Committee on Appropriations Subcommittee on Homeland Security held a hearing entitled "Privacy and Civil Rights in Homeland Security." The witnesses included Hugo Teufel III, the Chief Privacy Officer at DHS; Daniel Sutherland of the Office of Civil Rights and Civil Liberties at DHS; and the Government Accountability Office (GAO). Collectively they addressed some of the data mining activities being carried out by DHS, in particular the use of the Analysis, Dissemination, Visualization, Insight, and Semantic Enhancement (ADVISE) data mining tool, and the precautions taken by DHS to protect citizens' privacy and civil liberties.

On April 12, 2007, the Senate Committee on the Judiciary voted to approve a revised version of S. 236, the Data Mining Act of 2007. On June 4, 2007, the Committee reported the bill. With one exception, this revised version of S. 236 is substantively identical to data mining provision passed as Section 604 in S. 4, and later as Section 804 of P.L. 110-53 in July 2007 (discussed below). As passed by the Committee, S. 236 includes a provision regarding penalties for the unauthorized disclosure of classified information contained in the annex of any reports submitted to Congress.

On June 15, 2007, the House of Representatives passed H.R. 2638, concerning FY2008 appropriations for the Department of Homeland Security. The accompanying House Report (H.Rept. 110-181) includes language prohibiting funding for the Analysis, Dissemination, Visualization, Insight, and Semantic Enhancement (ADVISE) data mining program until DHS has completed a privacy impact assessment for the program. ADVISE is alternatively described as a technology framework, or a tool, for analyzing and visually representing large amounts of data. ADVISE is being developed by the Directorate for Science and Technology at DHS. The accompanying Senate Report (S.Rept. 110-84) for S. 1644, concerning FY2008 DHS appropriations, also includes similar language recommending that no funding be allocated for ADVISE until a program plan and privacy impact assessment is completed.

On July 9, 2007, the Senate took up H.R. 1, struck all language following the enacting clause, substituted the language of S. 4 as amended, and passed the bill by unanimous consent. Differences between H.R. 1 and S. 4 were resolved in conference later that month. The data mining provision that appeared as Section 604 in S. 4 was retained as Section 804 in the agreed upon bill. On July 26, 2007, the Senate agreed to the conference report (H.Rept. 110-259) in a 85-8 vote. On July 27, 2007, the House agreed to the conference report in a 371-40 vote. On August 3, 2007, the bill was signed into law by the President as P.L. 110-53.

For Further Reading

CRS Report RL32802, *Homeland Security: Air Passenger Prescreening and Counterterrorism*, by Bart Elias and William Krouse. Out of print; available from author (7-8679).

CRS Report RL32536, *Multi-State Anti-Terrorism Information Exchange (MATRIX)Pilot Project*, by William J. Krouse.

CRS Report RL30671, *Personal Privacy Protection: The Legislative Response*, by Harold C. Relyea. Out of print; available from author (7-8679).

CRS Report RL31730, *Privacy: Total Information Awareness Programs and Related Information Access, Collection, and Protection Laws*, by Gina Marie Stevens.

CRS Report RL3 1786, *Total Information Awareness Programs: Funding, Composition, and Oversight Issues*, by Amy Belasco.

DARPA, *Report to Congress Regarding the Terrorism Information Awareness Program*, May 20, 2003, [http://www.eff.org/Privacy/TIA/TIA-report.pdf].

Department of Defense, Office of the Inspector General, *Information Technology Management: Terrorism Information Awareness Program (D-2004-033)*, December 12, 2003 [http://www.dodig.osd.mil/audit/reports/FY04/04-03 3 .pdf].

Department of Homeland Security, Office of the Inspector General, *Survey of DHS Data Mining Activities (OIG-06-56)*, August 2006 [http://www.dhs.gov/xoig/assets/mgmtrpts/OIG_06-56_Aug06.pdf].

Department of Homeland Security, Office of Legislative Affairs, *Letter Report Pursuant to Section 804 of the Implementing Recommendations of the 9/11 Commission Act of 2007*, February 11, 2008, [http://www.dhs.gov/xlibrary/assets/privacy/privacy_rpt_datamining_2008.pdf].

Department of Homeland Security, Privacy Office, *2007 Data Mining Report: DHS Privacy Office Response to House Report 109-699*, July 6, 2007, [http://www.dhs.gov/xlibrary/assets/privacy/privacy_rpt_datamining_2007.pdf].

Department of Homeland Security, Privacy Office, *Report to the Public on the Transportation Security Administration's Secure Flight Program and Privacy Recommendations*, December 2006, [http://www.dhs.gov/xlibrary/assets/privacy/privacy-secure-flight-1 22006.pdf].

Department of Homeland Security, Privacy Office, *Report to the Public Concerning the Multistate Anti-Terrorism Information Exchange (MATRIX) Pilot Project*, December 2006, [http://www.dhs.gov/xlibrary/assets/privacy/privacy-secure-flight-1 22006.pdf].

Jeff Jonas and Jim Harper, *Effective Counterterrorism and the Limited Role of Predictive Data Mining*, CATO Institute Policy Analysis No. 584, December 11, 2006 [http://www.cato.org/pubs/pas/pa584.pdf].

Office of the Director of National Intelligence, *Data Mining Report*, February 1 5, 2008, [http://www.dni.gov/reports/data_mining_report_feb08.pdf].

References

[1] Two Crows Corporation, *Introduction to Data Mining and Knowledge Discovery, Third Edition* (Potomac, MD: Two Crows Corporation, 1999); Pieter Adriaans and Dolf Zantinge, *Data Mining* (New York: Addison Wesley, 1996).

[2] For a more technically-oriented definition of data mining, see [http://searchcrm .techtarget.com/gDefinition/0,294236,sid11_gci211901,00.html].

[3] John Makulowich, "Government Data Mining Systems Defy Definition," *Washington Technology*, 22 February 1999, [http://www.washingtontechnology.com/news/13_22/tech_ features/393-3 .html].

[4] Jiawei Han and Micheline Kamber, *Data Mining: Concepts and Techniques* (New York: Morgan Kaufmann Publishers, 2001), p. 7.

[5] Pieter Adriaans and Dolf Zantinge, *Data Mining* (New York: Addison Wesley, 1996), pp. 5-6.

[6] Ibid., p. 2.

[7] Two Crows Corporation, *Introduction to Data Mining and Knowledge Discovery, Third Edition* (Potomac, MD: Two Crows Corporation, 1999), p. 4.

[8] Ibid., p. 2.

[9] Ibid., p. 1.

[10] Jeff Jonas and Jim Harper, Effective Counterterrorism and the Limited Role of Predictive *Data Mining*, CATO Institute Policy Analysis No. 584, December 11, 2006 p. 8, [http://www.cato.org/pubs/pas/pa584.pdf].

[11] Two Crows Corporation, Introduction to Data Mining and Knowledge Discovery, Third Edition (Potomac, MD: Two Crows Corporation, 1999), p. 5; Patrick Dillon, Data Mining: Transforming Business Data Into Competitive Advantage and Intellectual Capital (Atlanta GA: The Information Management Forum, 1998), pp. 5-6.

[12] George Cahlink, "Data Mining Taps the Trends," *Government Executive Magazine*, October 1, 2000, [http://www.govexec.com/tech/articles/ 1000managetech.htm].

[13] Ibid.; for a more detailed review of the purpose for data mining conducted by federal departments and agencies, see U.S. General Accounting Office, *Data Mining: Federal Efforts Cover a Wide Range of Uses*, GAO Report GAO-04-548 (Washington: May 2004).

[14] This project was originally identified as the Total Information Awareness project until DARPA publicly renamed it the Terrorism Information Awareness project in May 2003. Section 8131 of the FY2004 Department of Defense Appropriations Act (P.L. 108-87) prohibited further funding of TIA as a whole, while allowing unspecified subcomponents of the TIA initiative to be funded as part of DOD's classified budget, subject to the provisions of the National Foreign Intelligence Program, which

restricts the processing and analysis of information on U.S. citizens. For further details regarding this provision, see CRS Report RL3 1805, *Authorization and Appropriations for FY2004: Defense*, by Amy Belasco and Stephen Daggett.

[15] DARPA "is the central research and development organization for the Department of Defense (DOD)" that engages in basic and applied research, with a specific focus on "research and technology where risk and payoff are both very high and where success may provide dramatic advances for traditional military roles and missions." [http://www.darpa.mil/]

[16] Department of Defense. May 20, 2003. Report to Congress Regarding the Terrorism Information Awareness Program, Executive Summary, p. 2.

[17] Department of Defense. May 20, 2003. Report to Congress Regarding the Terrorism Information Awareness Program, Detailed Information, p. 1 (emphasis added).

[18] Department of Defense, Office of the Inspector General. December 12, 2003. Information Technology Management: Terrorism Information Awareness Project (D2004- 033). p. 7.

[19] It is important to note that while DARPA's mission is to conduct research and development on technologies that can be used to address national-level problems, it would not be responsible for the operation of TIA, if it were to be adopted.

[20] For more details about the Terrorism Information Awareness program and related information and privacy laws, see CRS Report RL31730, *Privacy: Total Information Awareness Programs and Related Information Access, Collection, and Protection Laws*, by Gina Marie Stevens, and CRS Report RL3 1786, *Total Information Awareness Programs: Funding, Composition, and Oversight Issues*, by Amy Belasco.

[21] Department of Defense, DARPA, "Defense Advanced Research Project Agency's Information Awareness Office and Total Information Awareness Project," p. 1, [http://www.iwar.org.uk/news-archive/tia/iaotia.pdf].

[22] Ibid., p. 2.

[23] Although most of the TIA-related projects did involve some form of data collection, the primary purposes of some of these projects, such as war gaming, language translation, and biological agent detection, were less connected to data mining activities. For a description of these projects, see [http://www.fas.org/irp/agency/dod/poindexter.html].

[24] The text of Poindexter's presentation is available at [http://www.darpa.mil/ DARPATech2002/presentations/iao_pdf/speeches/POINDEXT.pdf]. The slide presentation of Poindexter's presentation is available at [http://www.darpa.mil/DARPATech2002/ presentations/iao_pdf/slides/PoindexterIAO.pdf].

[25] Shane Harris, "Counterterrorism Project Assailed By Lawmakers, Privacy Advocates," *Government Executive Magazine,* 25 November 2002, [http://www.govexec.com/ dailyfed/1 102/1 12502h1.htm].

[26] The original logo can be found at [http://www.thememoryhole.org/ policestate/iaologo.htm].

[27] The report is available at [http://www.eff.org/Privacy/TIA/TIA-report.pdf]. Some of the information required includes spending schedules, likely effectiveness of the program, likely impact on privacy and civil liberties, and any laws and regulations that may need to be changed to fully deploy TIA. If the report was not submitted within 90 days, funding for the TIA program could have been discontinued. For more details regarding this amendment, see CRS Report RL31786, *Total Information Awareness Programs: Funding, Composition, and Oversight Issues*, by Amy Belasco.

[28] For further details regarding this provision, see CRS Report RL3 1805 *Authorization and Appropriations for FY2004: Defense*, by Amy Belasco and Stephen Daggett.

[29] Department of Transportation, *White House Commission on Aviation and Security: The DOT Status Report,* February 1998, [http://www.dot.gov/affairs/whcoasas.htm].

[30] The Gore Commission was established by Executive Order 13015 on August 22, 1996, following the crash of TWA flight 800 in July 1996.

[31] White House Commission on Aviation Safety and Security: Final Report to President Clinton. February 12, 1997. [http://www.fas.org/irp/threat/21 2fin~1 .html].

[32] The docket can be found online at [http://dms.dot.gov/search /document.cfm ?documentid=57279&docketid=553 6].

[33] *Federal Register*, 64 (April 19,1999): 19220.

[34] U.S. General Accounting Office, Aviation Security: Computer-Assisted Passenger Prescreening System Faces Significant Implementation Challenges, GAO Report GAO-04- 385, February 2004, pp. 5-6.

[35] Transportation Security Administration, "TSA's CAPPS II Gives Equal Weight to Privacy, Security," Press Release, March 11, 2003, [http://www.tsa.gov/public/display ?theme=44&content=535].

[36] Robert O'Harrow, Jr., "Aviation ID System Stirs Doubt," *Washington Post*, 14 March 2003, p. A16.

[37] Transportation Security Administration, "TSA's CAPPS II Gives Equal Weight to Privacy, Security," Press Release, March 11, 2003, [http://www.tsa.gov/public/ display?theme=44&content=535].

[38] Sara Kehaulani Goo, "U.S. to Push Airlines for Passenger Records," *Washington Post*, January 12, 2004, p. A1.

[39] The Boycott Delta website is available at [http://www.boycottdelta.org].

[40] Don Phillips, "JetBlue Apologizes for Use of Passenger Records," *The Washington Post*, 20 September 2003, p. E1; Sara Kehaulani Goo, "TSA Helped JetBlue Share Data, Report Says," *Washington Post*, February 21, 2004, p. E1.

[41] Sara Kehaulani Goo, "Northwest Gave U.S. Data on Passengers," *Washington Post*, January 18, 2004, p. A1.

[42] Sara Kehaulani Goo, "American Airlines Revealed Passenger Data," *Washington Post*, April 10, 2004, p. D12.

[43] For the written responses to the committee's questions, see [http://www.epic.org/privacy/ airtravel/stone_answers.pdf]; Sara Kehaulani Goo, "Agency Got More Airline Records," *Washington Post*, June 24, 2004, p. A16.

[44] Some information, such as meal preferences, which could be used to infer religious affiliation, and health considerations will not be made available. Goo, Sara Kehaulani, "U.S., EU Will Share Passenger Records," *Washington Post*, May 29, 2004, p. A2.

[45] Department of Homeland Security, "Fact Sheet: US-EU Passenger Name Record Agreement Signed," May 28, 2004, [http://www.dhs.gov/dhspublic/display?content=365 1].

[46] *Federal Register*. Vol. 68 No. 148. August 1, 2003. p. 45266; U.S. General Accounting Office, *Aviation Security: Challenges Delay Implementation of Computer-Assisted Passenger Prescreening System*, GAO Testimony GAO-04-504T, March 17, 2004, p. 17

[47] U.S. General Accounting Office, Aviation Security: Challenges Delay Implementation of Computer-Assisted Passenger Prescreening System, GAO Testimony GAO-04-504T, March 17, 2004, p. 17.

[48] The eight issues included establishing an oversight board, ensuring the accuracy of the data used, conducting stress testing, instituting abuse

prevention practices, preventing unauthorized access, establishing clear policies for the operation and use of the system, satisfying privacy concerns, and created a redress process. U.S. General Accounting Office, *Aviation Security: Computer-Assisted Passenger Prescreening System Faces Significant Implementation Challenges*, GAO Report GAO-04-385, February 2004.

[49] U.S. Government Accountability Office, Aviation Security: Secure Flight Development and Testing Under Way, but Risks Should Be Managed as System is Further Developed, GAO Report GAO-05-356, March 2005.

[50] Ibid., p. 4; for a more detailed analysis of the Secure Flight program, see CRS Report RL32802, *Homeland Security: Air Passenger Screening and Counterterrorism*, by Bart Elias and William Krouse.

[51] U.S. General Accountability Office, Aviation Security: Significant Management Challenges May Adversely Affect the Implementation of the Transportation Security Administration's Secure Flight Program, GAO Testimony GAO-06-374T.

[52] U.S. General Accountability Office, Aviation Security: Management Challenges Remain for the Transportation Security Administration's Secure Flight Program, GAO Testimony GAO-06-864T.

[53] U.S. Department of Homeland Security, Privacy Office, *Report to the Public on the Transportation Security Administration's Secure Flight Program and Privacy Recommendations*, December 2006, p.13, [http://www.dhs.gov/xlibrary/assets/privacy/ privacy-secure-flight-1 22006.pdf].

[54] Eric Lipton, "U.S. Official Admits to Big Delay in Revamping No-Fly Program," *New York Times*, February 21, 2007, p. A17.

[55] Department of Homeland Security, Transportation Security Administration, "Privacy Act of 1974: Implementation of Exemptions; Secure Flight Records," 72 *Federal Register* 48397, August 23, 2007.

[56] Department of Homeland Security, Transportation Security Administration, "Privacy Act of 1974: System of Records; Secure Flight Records," 72 *Federal Register* 48392, August 23, 2007.

[57] See [http://www.tsa.gov/assets/pdf/pia_secureflight.pdf].

[58] Department of Homeland Security, Bureau of Customers and Border Protection, "Advance Electronic Transmission of Passenger and Crew Member Manifests for Commercial Aircraft and Vessels," 72 *Federal Register* 48320, August 23, 2007.

[59] Department of Homeland Security, Transportation Security Administration, "Secure Flight Program," 72 *Federal Register* 48356, August 23, 2007.
[60] Department of Homeland Security, Transportation Security Administration, "Secure Flight Program," 72 *Federal Register* 48356, August 23, 2007.
[61] Ibid., p. 48369.
[62] Ibid., p. 48364.
[63] Ibid., p. 48359.
[64] Ibid., p. 48363.
[65] Ibid., p. 48356.
[66] Department of Homeland Security, Transportation Security Administration, "Secure Flight Program," 72 *Federal Register* 60307, October 24, 2007.
[67] Department of Homeland Security, Transportation Security Administration, "Privacy Act of 1974: System of Records; Secure Flight Records," 72 *Federal Register* 63711, November 9, 2007.
[68] Department of Homeland Security, Transportation Security Administration, "Privacy Act of 1974: Implementation of Exemptions; Secure Flight Records," 72 *Federal Register* 63706, November 9, 2007.
[69] A copy of the presentation is available at [http://www.aclu.org/Files/OpenFile.cfm?id= 15813].
[70] Brian Bergstein, "Database Firm Tagged 120,000 Terrorism 'Suspects' for Feds," *The SunHerald*, May 20, 2004, [http://www.sunherald.com/mld/sunherald/business/technology/ 8715327.htm].
[71] The FDLE website is available at [http://www.fdle.state.fl.us/].
[72] The IIR website is available at [http://www.iir.com/].
[73] The MATRIX project website was deactivated at the conclusion of the pilot period. It was previously available at [http://www.matrix-at.org/].
[74] Information originally drawn from the MATRIX website, which is no longer available, at [http://www.matrix-at.org/FACTS_defined.htm].
[75] Ibid.
[76] Information originally drawn from the MATRIX website, which is no longer available, at [http://www.matrix-at.org/newsletter.pdf].
[77] Information originally drawn from the MATRIX website, which is no longer available, at [http://www.matrix-at.org/data_sources.htm].
[78] For a detailed description of RISS, see [http://www.iir.com/riss/] and [http://www.rissinfo.com/].
[79] [http://www.rissinfo.com/overview2.htm].

[80] John Schwartz, "Privacy Fears Erode Support for a Network to Fight Crime," *New York Times*, 15 March 2004, [http://www.nytimes.com/2004/03/15/technology/15matrix.html].

[81] Cynthia L. Webb, "Total Information Dilemma," *Washington Post*, May 27, 2004, http://www.washingtonpost.com/ac2/wp-dyn/A60986-2004May27?language=printer]; Lucy Morgan, "Ex-drug Runner Steps Aside," *St. Petersburg Times*, August 30, 2003, [http://www.sptimes.com/2003/08/30/State/Ex_drug_runner_steps_.shtml]; Bill Cotterell, and Nancy Cook Lauer, "Bush Defends Pick of Computer Firm, Former Leader's Background Raises Questions," *allahassee Democrat*, May 22, 2004, http://www.tallahassee.com/mld/tallahassee/news/local/8728776.htm].

[82] Welsh, William Welsh, "Feds Offer to Mend Matrix," *Washington Technology*, May 24, 2004, [http://www.washington technology.com/news/19_4/egov/23597-1.html].

[83] O'Harrow, Jr., Robert O'Harrow, Jr., "Anti-Terror Database Got Show at White House," *Washington Post*, May 21, 2004, p. A12.

[84] John Schwartz, "Privacy Fears Erode Support for a Network to Fight Crime," *New York Times*, March 15, 2004, [http://www.nytimes.com/2004/03/15/ technology/15matrix.html].

[85] For a more detailed discussion of Metcalfe's Law, see [http://searchnetworking .techtarget.com/sDefinition/0,,sid7_gci214115,00.html].

[86] The states that have reportedly decided to withdraw from the pilot project include Alabama, California, Georgia, Kentucky, Louisiana, New York, Oregon, South Carolina, Texas, Utah, and Wisconsin. Larry Greenemeier, "Two More States Withdraw From Database," *Information Week*, March 12, 2004, [http://www.informationweek.com/story/showArticle.jhtml?articleID=1 8312112]; Diane Frank, "Utah No Longer Part of MATRIX," *Federal Computer Week*, April 5, 2004, p. 14; Associated Press, "Two More States Withdraw From Controversial Database Program," *Star-Telegram*, March 12, 2004, [http://www.dfw.com/mld/dfw/business/8170978.htm? 1 c]; Associated Press, "Matrix Plan Fuels Privacy Fears," *Wired News*, February 2, 2004, [http://www.wired.com/news/business/ 0,1367,62141 ,00.html].

[87] Florida Department of Law Enforcement (FDLE). "News Release: MATRIX Pilot Project Concludes," April 15, 2005, [http://www.fdle.state.fl.us/press_releases/expired/2005/ 2005041 5_matrix_proj ect.html].

[88] Department of Defense, Special Defense Department Briefing, September 1, 2005, [http://www.defenselink.mil/transcripts/2005/ tr2005090 1 -3844.html].
[89] Shane Harris, "Homeland Security - Intelligence Designs," *National Journal*, December 3, 2005, [http://www.govexec.com/dailyfed/1205/ 120705nj 1 .htm].
[90] Erik Kleinsmith, Testimony before the Senate Committee on the Judiciary, *Able Danger and Intelligence Information Sharing*, September 21, 2005, [http://judiciary.senate.gov/ testimony.cfm?id=1 606&wit_id=4669].
[91] Department of Defense, Office of the Inspector General, "Alleged Misconduct by Senior DoD Officials Concerning the Able Danger Program and Lieutenant Colonel Anthony A. Shaffer, U.S. Army Reserve," Report of Investigation, September 18, 2006, [http://www.dodig.mil/fo/foia/ERR/ r_H05L9790521 7-PWH.pdf].
[92] A copy of the letter is available at [http://www.intelligence. senate.gov/abledanger.pdf].
[93] Department of Homeland Security, Office of the Secretary, "Privacy Act of 1974; System of Records," 71 *Federal Register* 64543, November 2, 2006.
[94] Department of Homeland Security, *Privacy Impact Assessment for the Automated Targeting System*, November 22, 2006, p.3, [http://www.dhs.gov/xlibrary/assets/privacy/ privacy_pia_cbp_ats.pdf].
[95] Department of Homeland Security, Office of the Secretary, "Privacy Act of 1974; U.S. Customs and Border Protection, Automated Targeting System, System of Records," 72 *Federal Register* 43650, August 6, 2007.
[96] Department of Homeland Security, Privacy Office, *2007 Data Mining* Report: DHS Privacy Office Response to House Report 109-699, July 6, 2007, [http://www.dhs.gov/xlibrary/assets/privacy/ privacy_rpt_ datamining_2007.pdf], p. 17.
[97] Ibid., p. 7 and p. 17, footnote 34.
[98] Department of Homeland Security, Office of the Secretary, "Privacy Act of 1974: Implementation of Exemptions; Automated Targeting System," 72 *Federal Register* 43567, August 6, 2007.
[99] Department of Homeland Security, Office of the Secretary, "Privacy Act of 1974; U.S. Customs and Border Protection, Automated Targeting System, System of Records," 72 *Federal Register* 43650, August 6, 2007.

[100] See [http://www.dhs.gov/xlibrary/assets/privacy/privacy_ pia_cbp_ atsupdate.pdf].

[101] Department of Homeland Security, Office of the Secretary, "Privacy Act of 1974: mplementation of Exemptions; Automated Targeting System," 72 *Federal Register* 43567, August 6, 2007.

[102] Department of Homeland Security, Office of the Secretary, "Privacy Act of 1974; U.S. Customs and Border Protection, Automated Targeting System, System of Records," 72 *Federal Register* 43650, August 6, 2007.

[103] Peter Baker, "President Says He Ordered NSA Domestic Spying," *The Washington Post*, 18 December 2005, p. A1; Walter Pincus, "NSA Gave Other U.S. Agencies Information From Surveillance," *The Washington Post*, January 1, 2006, p. A8.

[104] President George W. Bush, "President's Radio Address," December 17, 2005, [http://www.whitehouse.gov/news/releases/2005/1 2/2005121 7.html].

[105] Ibid.

[106] U.S. Department of Justice, "The NSA Program to Detect and Prevent Terrorist Attacks Myth v. Reality," January 27, 2006, [http://www.usdoj .gov/opa/documents/nsa_myth_v_ reality.pdf].

[107] The Honorable Alberto Gonzalez, Testimony before the Senate Committee on the Judiciary, *Wartime Executive Power and the NSA 's Surveillance Authority*, February 6, 2006, [http://judiciary.senate.gov/ testimony.cfm?id=1 727&wit_id=3936].

[108] Leslie Cauley, "NSA has Massive Database of Americans' Phone Calls," *USA Today*, May 11, 2006, p. 1A; Stephen Dinan and Charles Hurt, "Bush Denies Report of 'Trolling' by NSA," *The Washington Times*, May 12, 2006, p. A1; Barton Gellman and Arshad Mohammed, "Data on Phone Calls Monitored," *The Washington Post*, May 12, 2006, p. A1.

[109] BellSouth Corporation, "BellSouth Statement on Government Data Collection," May 15, 2006, [http://bellsouth.mediaroom.com/ index.php?s= press_releases&item=2860].

[110] Verizon, "Verizon Issues Statement on NSA News Media Coverage," May 16, 2006, [http://newscenter.verizon.com/proactive/newsroom/ release.vtml?id=93450&PROACTIVE_ID=cecdc6cdc8c8cbcacbc5cecfcfcfc 5cecdcecfc6cacacac6c7c5cf].

[111] Barton Gellman and Arshad Mohammed, "Data on Phone Calls Monitored," *The Washington Post*, May 12, 2006, p. A1.

[112] Senator Patrick Leahy, "Letter of Attorney General Alberto Gonzales to the Chairman and Ranking Member of the Senate Judiciary Committee ordered printed without objection," remarks in the Senate, *Congressional Record*, daily edition, vol. 153 (January 17, 2001), pp. S646-S647.

[113] [https://rrc.mitre.org/cfp06.pdf].

[114] Shane Harris, "NSA Spy Program Hinges on State-of-the-Art Technology," *Government Executive Magazine*, January 20, 2006, [http://www.govexec.com/dailyfed/0106/ 01 2006nj 1 .htm]; Wilson P. Dizard III, "NSA Searches for Novel Intel Answers in the Glass Box," *Government Computer News*, June 20, 2005, [http://www.gcn.com/24_1 5/news/ 36139-1.html].

[115] ARDA's website was previously available at [http://www.ic-arda.org].

[116] Technology and Privacy Advisory Committee, Department of Defense. *Safeguarding Privacy in the Fight Against Terrorism*, March 2004, p. 40.

[117] Ibid., p. 39.

[118] Drew Clark, "Privacy Experts Differ on Merits of Passenger-Screening Program," *Government Executive Magazine*, November 21, 2003, [http://www.govexec.com/dailyfed/ 1103/1 12103td2.htm].

[119] The report is available at [http://www.eff.org/Privacy/TIA/TIA-report.pdf].

[120] For more details regarding this amendment, see CRS Report RL31786, *Total Information Awareness Programs: Funding, Composition, and Oversight Issues*, by Amy Belasco.

[121] For further details regarding this provision, see CRS Report RL3 1 805, *Authorization and Appropriations for FY2004: Defense*, by Amy Belasco and Stephen Daggett.

[122] Section 519 of P.L. 108-90 specifically identifies eight issues that TSA must address before it can spend funds to deploy or implement CAPPS II on other than a test basis. These include 1. establishing a system of due process for passengers to correct erroneous information; 2. assess the accuracy of the databases being used; 3. stress test the system and demonstrate the efficiency and accuracy of the search tools; 4. establish and internal oversight board; 5. install operational safeguards to prevent abuse; 6. install security measures to protect against unauthorized access by hackers or other intruders; 7. establish policies for effective oversight of system use and operation; and 8. address any privacy concerns related to the system.

[123] General Accounting Office, Aviation Security: Computer-Assisted Passenger Prescreening System Faces Significant Implementation Challenges, GAO-04-385, February 2004, p. 4.

[124] Ibid.

[125] Witnesses testifying at the hearing included Florida State Senator Paula Dockery, Dr. Jen Que Louie representing Nautilus Systems, Inc., Mark Forman representing OMB, Gregory Kutz representing GAO, and Jeffrey Rosen, an Associate Professor at George Washington University Law School.

[126] H.R. 1502 was referred to the Subcommittee on Immigration, Border Security, and Claims on May 10, 2005, and later discharged by the subcommittee on July 8, 2005.

[127] See p. 180.

[128] Ibid., p. 117. The DHS Privacy Office delivered the requested report to Congress on July 6, 2007. A copy of the report is available at [http://www.dhs.gov/xlibrary/assets/privacy/privacy_rpt_datamining_2007.pdf].

[129] On April 12, 2007, the Committee voted to approve a revised version of S. 236, which was sent to the full Senate. A description of this version of the bill is discussed later in the chronology of this section of the report.

[130] Witnesses testifying at the hearing included former Representative Robert Barr of Liberty Strategies, LLC; James Carafano of the Heritage Foundation; Jim Harper of the CATO Institute; Leslie Harris of the Center for Democracy and Technology; and Kim Taipale of the Center for Advanced Studies in Science and Technology.

[131] *Congressional Record*, vol. 153, March 6, 2007, p. S2670.

[132] *Congressional Record*, vol. 153, March 8, 2007, p. S2949.

[133] Ibid.

In: Digital Surveillance
Editor: J. G. Massingale, pp. 65-83
ISBN: 978-1-60692-312-2

Chapter 3

DATA MINING REPORT*

Office of the Director of National Intelligence

15 February 2008

The Office of the Director of National Intelligence (ODNI) is pleased to provide to the Congress this chapter pursuant to Section 804 of the Implementing the Recommendations of the 9/11 Commission Act of 2007, entitled The Federal Agency Data Mining Reporting Act of 2007 ("Data Mining Reporting Act"). The Data Mining Reporting Act requires "the head of each department or agency of the Federal Government" that is engaged in activities defined as "data mining" to report on such activities to the Congress.

SCOPE

This chapter covers the data mining activities of all elements of the ODNI. Constituent elements of the Intelligence Community are reporting their data mining activities through their own departments or agencies. This chapter covering ODNI activities is unclassified and has been made available to the public through the ODNI' s website. A classified annex has also been prepared and has been transmitted to the appropriate Congressional committees.

* This is an edited, excerpted and augmented edition of a Office of the Director of National Intelligence publication.

Other Intelligence Community elements

The ODNI' s Civil Liberties and Privacy Office (CLPO) has requested that civil liberties and privacy officers within the Intelligence Community disclose their data mining activities to the ODNI and provide copies of any reports submitted in response to the Data Mining Reporting Act.

Definition of "data mining"

The Data Mining Report Act defines "data mining" as "a program involving pattern-based queries, searches or other analyses of 1 or more electronic databases" in order to "discover or locate a predictive pattern or anomaly indicative of terrorist or criminal activity . . . ."

The limitation to predictive, "pattern-based" data mining is significant because analysis performed within the ODNI and its constituent elements for counterterrorism and similar purposes is often performed using various types of link analysis tools. These tools start with a known or suspected terrorist or other subject of foreign intelligence interest and use various methods to uncover links between that known subject and potential associates or other persons with whom that subject is or has been in contact.

The Data Mining Reporting Act does not include such analyses within its definition of "data mining" because such analyses are not "pattern-based." Rather, these analyses rely on inputting the "personal identifiers of a specific individual, or inputs associated with a specific individual or group of individuals," which is excluded from the definition of "data mining" under the Act.

ODNI Data Mining Activities

The ODNI's Office of Science and Technology's Intelligence Advanced Research Projects Activity (IARPA [1]) has a portfolio of research projects, some of which include the exploration of techniques that could be applied to data mining. These projects are research projects and their activities are being conducted for research purposes. They have not been deployed for use in any operational or other real life environments.

Results from such research projects may in the future be incorporated into operational programs employing data mining technology within the ODNI, the

Intelligence Community, or other parts of the United States government, subject to appropriate legal, privacy, civil liberties and policy safeguards. Because of the potential privacy and civil liberties impact of the development of these technologies, IARPA is also specifically researching the use of technology to better protect privacy in light of these challenges.

Overview of Incisive Analysis Area

The Intelligence Advanced Research Projects Activity (IARPA) funds cutting edge research to address difficult and complex intelligence community challenges. Today's intelligence analysts must wade through an exponentially increasing amount of data (both classified and open source) to uncover potentially key nuggets of valuable information in time for them to be transformed into timely, actionable intelligence.

IARPA's Incisive Analysis efforts are comprised of research projects designed to address this challenge by harnessing advanced analytic tools to aid the human analyst in looking through large volumes of data to uncover the information that is most relevant in a timely fashion. Some of these projects include elements that meet the Data Mining Reporting Act's definition of data mining.

IARPA activities are by nature highly experimental and pioneering and are designed to produce new capabilities not even imagined by the operational agencies it serves. The typical context behind an IARPA project involves the demonstration of a never-beforeseen capability, the establishment of relevant technical metrics for this capability, a baseline comparison (if possible) with existing legacy solution(s), and the tracking of such performance metrics throughout the life of the project. Because IARPA pursues high-risk, high-payoff solutions, its projects do not necessarily result in deployable technologies. When they do, additional steps are needed to transform the results of IARPA research into real world applications, which may be different from what was originally envisioned.

As a result, the activities within IARPA's Incisive Analysis projects that meet the "data mining" definition of the Data Mining Reporting Act will generally not be at a level of technological readiness that permits an accurate judgment as to their efficacy and generally will not have an existing basis for determining that a pattern or anomaly is indicative of terrorist activity. Indeed, the very purpose of the Incisive Analysis projects, as with all of IARPA's research, is to answer these questions in order to determine whether such technology is promising enough to warrant additional investment to develop tools that could be deployed within the Intelligence Community.

INCISIVE ANALYSIS PROJECTS: DETAILED RESPONSE

The Data Mining Reporting Act requires detailed information regarding data mining activities. Some information is classified and a classified annex to this chapter has been prepared and made available to appropriate Congressional committees.

(A) A thorough description of the data mining activity, its goals, and, where appropriate, the target dates for the deployment of the data mining activity.

In order to deal with the challenge of addressing the exponential growth of information faced by the intelligence analysts, IARPA has created the Incisive Analysis portfolio, an ensemble of advanced research projects dedicated to achieving the DNI goals of creating a culture of collaboration, fostering collection and analytic transformation, and accelerating information sharing.

The Incisive Analysis portfolio does not focus on data mining *per se,* but certain projects within that portfolio are researching technologies that do meet the definition of data mining These are:

- *Knowledge Discovery and Dissemination (KDD).* KDD is seeking ways to coordinate access to and effectively exploit multiple, lawfully-collected data sources across the disparate intelligence community agencies.

o KDD research is not operationally engaged in discovering patterns of behavior in data that are indicative of criminal or terrorist groups. At a pure research level, one effort attempts to match known patterns of deception as provided by subject matter experts in foreign intelligence data.

o A few of the tools being developed by KDD may be used in the future for the conduct of data mining as defined by the Act. These include network tomography, predictive analysis, and hypothesis generation and validation tools.

o Some of the KDD tools are installed in a number of Intelligence Community Science and Technology (IC S&T) offices for testing and evaluation. Tools may be transitioned for operational use in accordance with KDD's plan to develop alliances with other IC S&T programs within the next year. Any transition resulting in operational use will coordinate with the civil liberties and privacy protection mechanisms of the receiving agency prior to implementation.

- o KDD is planning additional collaboration with the Department of Homeland Security (DHS) and law enforcement organizations by using a test and evaluation center to test analytic tools.

- The *Tangram* project is intended to evaluate the efficacy and intelligence value of a terrorism threat surveillance and warning system concept. Tangram explores the viability of a "surveillance and warning" system that will (i) report the threat likelihood of *known* threat entities, and (ii) serve to discover and report the threat likelihood of *unexpected* threat entities.

- o The experimental methodology includes continuously assessing the information we have about known threat entities. This assessment function would not necessarily involve data mining because known entities would be the subjects of the assessment. However, Tangram is evaluating the viability of pattern-based detection methods that could reveal a change in the threat likelihood of a known individual. We envision three areas where data mining techniques could potential improve Tangram performance: (a) overcoming common data problems, such as sparseness, incompleteness or incorrectness; (b) assessing multiple entity threat hypotheses; and (c) providing warning of unexpected threat entities. Areas (a) and (b) are scientifically proven techniques, while area (c) is an important research area of the project.

- The *Video Analysis and Content Extraction (VACE)* project seeks to automate what is now a very tedious, generally human-powered process of reviewing video for content that is potentially of intelligence value. In general, VACE will involve subject-based queries of video databases that do not meet the definition of data mining However, two aspects of the VACE program involve possible use of pattern-based data mining technologies.

- VACE conducts research in computer vision and machine learning topics such as (a) object detection, tracking, event detection and understanding, (b) scene classification, recognition and modeling, (c) intelligent content services such as indexing, video browsing, summarization, content browsing, video mining, and change detection.
- Application of these techniques to pattern-based problems includes (1) an effort seeking to automate processing of surveillance cameras, such as might be found in public transit terminals, to determine anomalous behavior, and (2) an effort that searches video databases, such as broadcast news video archives, to retrieve events such as bombings or beheadings where the query was not subject-based or seeded with a personal identifier.

- The *ProActive Intelligence (PAINT)* project seeks to study the dynamics of complex intelligence targets (inclusive of terrorist organizations) by examining patterns of causal relationships that are indicative of nefarious activity.

  - PAINT does not specifically aim to uncover patterns or anomalies suggestive of terrorist or criminal activities directly; therefore it is not related to the definition of data mining under the Act. However, future applications may have a tangential connection, so for completeness, it has been included.

- *Reynard* is a seedling effort to study the emerging phenomenon of social (particularly terrorist) dynamics in virtual worlds and large-scale online games and their implications for the Intelligence Community.

  - The cultural and behavioral norms of virtual worlds and gaming are generally unstudied. Therefore, Reynard will seek to identify the emerging social, behavioral and cultural norms in virtual worlds and gaming environments. The project would then apply the lessons learned to determine the feasibility of automatically detecting suspicious behavior and actions in the virtual world.
  - If it shows early promise, this small seedling effort may increase its scope to a full project.

Because application of results from these research projects may ultimately have implications for privacy and civil liberties, IARPA is also investing in projects that develop privacy protecting technologies *(cf.,* Section E - *Focus Area: Privacy Protecting Technologies)*

(B) A thorough description of the data mining technology that is being used or will be used, including the basis for determining whether a particular pattern or anomaly is indicative of terrorist or criminal activity.

IARPA conducts advanced research projects that explore new concepts and technologies. Although researchers in each of the Incisive Analysis projects that involve data mining activities have articulated sound reasons why they believe their technological approaches could be successful in identifying patterns or anomalies that could be useful to the Intelligence Community in discovering terrorist, criminal or other activities of interest, they usually do not have a specific, documented basis for determining whether a particular pattern or anomaly is indicative of specific activity (e.g., terrorism, criminal acts, etc.) In fact, one of the goals of these projects, as with all IARPA programs, is to create a basis for quantitative measurements.

- Knowledge Discovery and Dissemination (KDD).

  - Most tools that researchers are developing in the KDD program do not involve pattern-based data mining. However, some tools have been developed to discover patterns associated with deceptive behavior in groups using an analytic technique called network tomography. This tool looks for deception patterns in large databases. Other tools have been designed for predictive analysis, attempting to identify the next step in an emerging pattern, and hypothesis generation, seeking to provide possible explanations for observed anomalous patterns.

- *Tangram* is seeking to demonstrate the feasibility and intelligence value of a semi-autonomous terrorist threat assessment system concept. Its most immediate objective is to assess the threat likelihood of known threat entities. The simplest of methods would be initiated by a search for information about the specific entity However, a surveillance and warning system must also provide warnings where 1) the data are sparse, incomplete or erroneous, and 2) the threats are assessed across multiple lines of inquiry that individually would not reveal an entity's threat likelihood. Pattern-based data mining methods have proven effective at compensating for common data issues and fusing multi-sensor data to produce warnings. Tangram hopes to capitalize on these methods to improve its overall intelligence value as a function of true positives and false positives. Under these conditions Tangram will evaluate the efficacy of data mining methods.

- o Tangram will take advantage of research from IARPA's Privacy Protecting Technologies and KDD projects in addition to the tools that have been tested on the Research and Development Experimental Collaboration (RDEC) testing platform.[2]
- o A significant aspect of Tangram's research is discovering highly reliable threat patterns and statistics that will provide reliable warnings. Consequently, Tangram has no pre-existing patterns that have been applied to real intelligence data.
- o Because most of Tangram's computational methods have been successfully used for niche applications within the Intelligence Community and in commercial applications, Tangram researchers believe there is a proven basis for continuing to explore whether aggregations of subject-based and pattern-based methods could provide highly reliable warnings..

- *Video Analysis and Content Extraction (VACE)* seeks to dramatically increase analyst efficiency in processing video content. While VACE is not a data mining project *per se,* two aspects of VACE could involve pattern-based searches of video content for indications of possible terrorist or other criminal activity.

- o VACE is developing advanced video searching capabilities that could involve looking for particular patterns that might indicate a broadcast of terrorist events *(e.g.,* bombings, beheadings).
- o VACE has developed a Video Event Manager that permits analysts to find a particular event within video, such as an event that has possible security significance — for example, a person is observed entering a restricted area or leaves a bag in a public place.

- *ProActive Intelligence (PAINT)* studies the dynamics of complex intelligence targets, such as terrorist organizations, and employs models of causal relationships that are designed to increase analyst efficiency.

- o As noted in section (A), PAINT does not specifically aim to uncover patterns or anomalies suggestive of terrorist or criminal activities directly; therefore it is not related to the definition of data mining under the Act. However, future applications may have a tangential connection, so for completeness, it has been included.
- o *Reynard* is a small and highly exploratory seedling project which seeks to identify the emerging social, behavioral, and cultural norms in virtual worlds and gaming environments. If successful, Reynard may be expanded to a full-scale project.

(C) A thorough description of the data sources that are being or will be used.

Most of the projects within the Incisive Analysis area that involve data mining make use of the unique testing and evaluation capabilities and structured databases of the Research and Development Experimental Collaboration (RDEC) network. The RDEC network provides access to data from a number of classified databases containing lawfully collected foreign intelligence information. They have been copied and selected for inclusion within the RDEC network to permit testing and evaluation of new and promising analytical tools without any danger that the tools would damage or corrupt the data.

A listing of these databases is found in the classified appendix to this chapter.

KDD relies on research partners who develop analytic tools in accordance with research protocols that do not make data available in bulk form to IARPA. IARPA requires its partners to take steps to minimize the information provided in research results, even though many of these data sets are publicly available. This may require, for example, that partners report their findings in aggregate form *(e.g..,* without reporting any personally identifying information). Within the Intelligence Community, validated KDD tools are being tested with data sources associated with the counter-terrorism and counter-WMD missions to ensure robustness and ease of use.

All data sources used by the Tangram program since its inception have been synthetic, *i.e.,* fabricated simulations of real intelligence data. Tangram researchers anticipate using RDEC data in the future.

The video data used by the VACE program consists of lawfully collected data from public places outside the United States. Additional data sources used for testing are the National Institute of Standards and Technology (NIST) Video Retrieval (TRECVID) data, which are simulated video content created by volunteers specifically for research purposes.

PAINT uses lawfully collected foreign intelligence information for research purposes.

Reynard will conduct unclassified research in a public virtual world environment. The research will use publicly available data and will begin with observational studies to establish baseline normative behaviors.

An assessment of the efficacy or likely efficacy of the data mining activity in providing accurate information consistent with and valuable to the stated goals and plans for the use or development of the data mining activity.

Researchers have sound reasons for believing that their approaches have the potential to develop real world applications that will be effective in achieving their stated goals. Because Incisive Analysis programs are ongoing research, the projects are largely designed precisely to determine whether and how effective each of the analytical tools, including pattern-based tools, may be.

After a measurement system is developed based upon the capability in question, each data mining-related activity within IARPA will be compared with the systems in use by the Intelligence Community today to determine whether the capabilities developed by IARPA provide faster and more accurate information than traditional approaches. Processes will be carefully measured throughout the life of each project.

Even as researchers study how effective their proposed approaches are, they will coordinate with the IARPA's privacy protecting technologies project. This coordination will help researchers to determine how to incorporate additional privacy protecting technologies within the analytic tools they are developing. Coordination with the privacy protecting technologies project will enable researchers to assess whether such tools can be incorporated into their projects while preserving or even enhancing the efficacy of those tools in achieving their mission of enhancing intelligence analysis.

An assessment of the impact or likely impact of the implementation of the data mining activity on the privacy and civil liberties of individuals, including a thorough description of the actions that are being taken or will be taken with regard to the property, privacy, or other rights or privileges of any individual or individuals as a result of the implementation of the data mining activity.

The data mining activities that are part of the research projects within IARPA's Incisive Analysis portfolio could potentially impact the privacy or civil liberties of individuals if they are successfully transitioned to an operational partner without careful consideration of these issues. IARPA's privacy protecting technologies initiative[3], and the related work being sponsored by some individual projects, will ensure that the technologies developed by IARPA to serve national security ends do so through means that are both constitutionally valid and privacy enabling.

IARPA's privacy protecting technologies initiative is based in part on a unique collaboration of government experts, private sector experts, and privacy advocates at a series of workshops jointly sponsored by IARPA and the ODNI Civil Liberties and Privacy Office (CLPO) in the fall of 2006. These workshops examined an array of challenges to privacy posed by emerging technologies and government needs for information for intelligence and counterterrorism purposes. Experts suggested a variety of path breaking and innovative approaches to applying technology to these problems, and IARPA developed the privacy protecting technologies initiative to jump start research in the most promising areas.

In short, IARPA believes that the privacy and civil liberties of individuals will be well preserved with careful oversight of the projects and responsible consideration of privacy and civil liberties in the decision whether and how to deploy any resulting technologies. IARPA intends on maintaining its long-term relationship with the ODNI CLPO for the purpose of validating that its research agenda is consistent with the protection of individual privacy and civil liberties.

Focus Area: Privacy Protecting Technologies

This IARPA focus area seeks innovative technologies that can advance both the security and privacy of information collected, processed, and held for intelligence community purposes. In many cases, these two properties are well aligned. Good privacy policy calls for limiting use or retention of data beyond the purposes for which it is collected. This policy is also good for security, in that it limits what can be compromised. Technologies that promote the responsible handling of private data can also help build public confidence in the process.

Accountability, privacy, information sharing, and the technologies that promote them often overlap and display complex interrelationships in the private sector. For example, many enterprises collect information that can be used to identify individuals (personally identifiable information, or PII) in order to be able to conduct business with their customers. The customer must be willing to share some information (PII, in particular) with the enterprise in order to obtain desired services. As the enterprise wants to hold the customer accountable for the cost of services it provides, the customer wants to hold the enterprise accountable for providing the service and also for protecting the private information the enterprise holds. The enterprise may provide this accountability to the customer by using privacy protecting technologies, including technologies to assure that private information flows only where policy permits. The issues grow more complex when one enterprise deals with another either on behalf of a customer or on its own account. When the enterprise outsources or subcontracts, for example, the enterprise must assure that any PII conveyed to the subcontractor continues to be handled according to the applicable policies.

The data collected and held by the intelligence community and used to alert national leaders and to understand global affairs must be handled in accordance with many governing laws, regulations, policies and procedures that continue to evolve in response to public concerns both about privacy preservation and national security. Technologies are needed that can help assure that publicly agreed-upon policies are applied effectively and routinely. This assurance needs to be in place in order to facilitate legitimate, controlled sharing of information among the government organizations, including federal, state, local, and tribal entities, and also sharing with other countries and governments. Since any mechanism may be abused by authorized users, the technology also needs to resist insider threats and to help establish accountability for violations.

IARPA is evaluating proposals for research in these general areas of concern:

- Accuracy. The ability to review records and enter corrections or at least contest the entries is a conventional component of fair information practice Like the data in a credit report, intelligence data can be incorrect. Unlike credit data, however, it may be impractical or infeasible to permit the subject of the intelligence data to review it and enter corrections. For example, these cases include mistaken identification of an individual with a person who is on a watch list, or cases where an individual is correctly identified but has been mistakenly entered into a database or placed on a watch list. Not only facts, but the deductions and analyses based upon them, are at issue. One might imagine a system which, once an error of fact is detected, could more easily identify where that fact had been used and flag or roll back the reports needing correction. Methods for extracting meaning from content are not the concern here; the focus is on how to retract erroneous data and the inferences based on those erroneous data. Can new technologies help solve these problems without revealing sensitive information about sources and methods?
- Access. Just as sensitive corporate information may be revealed to litigants as part of the discovery process when a lawsuit is underway, information about an individual that would ordinarily be private may

legitimately be disclosed to investigators if the individual is the subject of an authorized investigation. If that information is in a database with the information of many other individuals, it may be inappropriate to (a) search all of the other data and (b) to reveal the search criteria (i.e., aliases for the individual or information that distinguishes the individual from other individuals with similar identifiers) to the holder of the database.

- Accountability. Accountability is a key tool to help assure that those entrusted with special privileges for data access use those privileges responsibly and also to assure that they can be credited with doing so. In some cases, a key part of the control regime may involve assuring that those accessing data can be held accountable for complying with the applicable rules and restrictions. Effective accountability measures can serve as a crucial deterrent to misbehavior. Audit controls can be effective in this context; completeness and integrity of the audit trail will be primary concerns.

Technology areas of particular interest include (but are not limited to) the following:

- Secure multi party function evaluation. While the mathematics of this technology has been studied for some time, practical applications have been lacking. Projects that can demonstrate how this technology could be applied to problems of realistic scale and complexity will be of interest. For example, agencies at different levels of the U.S. government, as well as selected foreign government and private sector entities, are all interested in comparing intelligence information concerning terrorist financing, yet these entities may be unwilling or unable to disclose their own detailed information for fear of violating privacy rules or compromising sources and methods. Secure multi-party function evaluation might provide a way for such entities to cooperate in computing the results regarding such financial flows without either sharing the information with each other or resorting to a trusted third party to compute it for them.
- Entity disambiguation methods. Innovative techniques that improve the precision with which one individual (perhaps with the same name or other identifier) can be distinguished from another and can be correctly associated with some set of data are of high interest. For example, during the course of an individual's security adjudication process, an

investigator finds records containing names that are variations of the subject's name (e.g., John, Jon, Johnny, Jack). The adjudicator must ensure that all records pertaining to the subject are examined while records containing the same name variants, but unrelated to the subject, are excluded.

- Applications of non-monotonic logic. Applications of non-monotonic logic to databases of significant size and complexity may be useful. For example, such applications could aid in locating and purging data that -- some time after collection -- are determined to be incorrect. Further, techniques that can automatically locate (and possibly retract) information or reports inferred or derived from incorrect data will be of interest. For example, a source deemed credible is later determined to be unreliable. Enough time has passed that intelligence from this source has been used in numerous analyses and cited in many reports and briefings. Technologies have been developed that can link documents, and even portions of documents, within a limited and controlled context (for example a single unified system using a common document processing system). A challenge is to use the power of non-monotonic logic to facilitate the automatic or semi-automatic retraction of inferences that have been made across a wide range of document types and formats.
- Rules-based access enforcement. Many rules, including rules designed to protect the privacy of U.S. persons, govern the accesses that a member of the Intelligence Community may make to various databases. Enforcement of these rules by requiring prior human review of every record before granting some level of access may be impracticable, but auditing of accesses can be used to complement enforcement. Automated checking of access rules against the audited data can be used to highlight potential abuses. Techniques for effectively checking realistic access sets against realistic rule bases will be of interest. For example, consider a financial records system that normally enforces specific access rules for access to customer data, but also supports special emergency access to sensitive financial data by law enforcement or intelligence personnel. Automated validation of the emergency access patterns after the fact could provide a strong deterrent for abuse.
- Private information retrieval (PIR). The ability to query a database without revealing to the operator of the database the search criteria or the data retrieved can prevent a database operator from making potentially injurious inferences about the subject of the search terms. PIR has been much researched but so far has not been reduced to practice. Techniques

that hold promise for making PIR applicable in a realistic context will be of interest. For example, suppose a mining company wishes to outsource the storage of voluminous mineral exploration data. The company also wishes to make queries against the data to look for promising areas to develop, yet the queries themselves can reveal the geographic areas of interest, and this information would be valuable to a competitor. So the company is only willing to outsource the storage to a firm that can guarantee the queries will not be revealed. The outsourcing company could potentially use PIR as a means of assuring its customers that it will not (cannot) compromise the data or the queries. Can private information retrieval technologies scale to deal with a global database of images?

- Anonymous matching. This technique, sometimes called private matching, and considered a special case of secure multiparty function evaluation, permits comparisons of multiple sets of data under the control of different parties while revealing selected data only (or no data at all) to the parties involved. It can protect privacy by shielding the identities of persons in the searched database from human review until, with a high probability, they match specific criteria. At this point, and with appropriate legal authority, some or all related data might be individually reviewed. Some products now incorporate techniques for exact matching, but matching that supports a "closeness" metric rather than a simple Boolean match is a research topic at present. Techniques that significantly advance the state of the art in this area would be of interest. For example, watch lists for suspected terrorists are clearly sensitive information, so governments are unwilling to release them publicly. The airline companies are similarly reluctant to provide unfettered access to their databases of passenger lists to governments. Effective techniques for anonymous matching could support the interests of both parties.

Assessing the effectiveness of a particular privacy protecting technology in a particular context can be a difficult problem in itself. Research that supports evaluation of the strength of a particular mechanism — how easily it may be bypassed or under what conditions it may leak information — will be of particular interest.

(F) A list and analysis of the laws and regulations that govern the information being or to be collected, reviewed, gathered, analyzed, or used in conjunction with the data mining activity, to the extent applicable in the context of the data mining activity.

Most of the information contained in the RDEC network and other lawfully collected intelligence information used by IARPA for test purposes consists of information about non-United States persons, *i.e.,* foreign citizens who are not permanent United States residents. Any information about U.S. persons contained within intelligence databases is governed by Executive Order 12,333, "United States Intelligence Activities," which governs the collection, retention and dissemination of information by the Intelligence Community that may include U.S. person information.

E.O. 12,333 requires each element of the Intelligence Community to maintain procedures, approved by the Attorney General, governing the collection, retention and dissemination of U.S. person information. These procedures limit the type of information that may be collected, retained or disseminated to the categories listed in part 2.3 of E.O. 12,333. For example, information that is publicly available or that constitutes foreign intelligence or counterintelligence may be collected, retained or disseminated.

The RDEC network databases generally consist of information collected and retained by elements of the Intelligence Community within the Department of Defense. As a result, the information within the RDEC network complies with Department of Defense regulation 5240.1, which is unclassified and governs all DOD intelligence activities. Implementing regulations and directives serve to protect the privacy of U.S. persons whose information may have been incidentally obtained in the course of foreign intelligence collection. For example, if the identity of a U.S. person is not needed to assess or understand foreign intelligence, that identity will be replaced with a generic term such as "U.S. person."

In addition to classified data sources, IARPA projects make some use of publicly available information. As described above, such information may be collected, retained or disseminated under E.O. 12,333 for lawful purposes related to IARPA's mission. Even in the case of such information, however, IARPA researchers have carefully coordinated their activities with the ODNI's Civil Liberties and Privacy Office to assess whether to use open source information that may pose real or perceived privacy or civil liberties risks.

The video data used by the VACE program consists of lawfully collected data from public places outside the United States and from volunteers specifically for research purposes. As a result, its use is consistent with E.O. 12,333.

In addition to E.O. 12,333, personal data retrieved by the name or identifier of a U.S. person must comply with the Privacy Act. However, the IARPA data sources generally consist of non-U.S. person intelligence information and incidentally collected U.S. person information is only retained consistent with E.O. 12,333.

Because IARPA does not retrieve information from these data sources using any personal identifiers associated with a U.S. person, IARPA does not maintain a system of records under the Privacy Act for these research purposes.

(G) A thorough discussion of the policies, procedures, and guidelines that are in place or that are to be developed and applied in the use of such data mining activity in order to— (i) protect the privacy and due process rights of individuals, such as redress procedures; and(ii) ensure that only accurate and complete information is collected, reviewed, gathered, analyzed, or used, and guard against any harmful consequences of potential inaccuracies.

Until the projects result in deployable technologies, it is difficult to assess the real and practical impact of the data mining activity on actual privacy and civil liberties interests. While one could imagine possible implications of successful research in each of the Incisive Analysis projects, the actual impact could be quite different depending on what technology actually results from the research and the context in which a given technology is deployed.

The intelligence community has in place a robust protective infrastructure. It consists of a core set of U.S. person rules derived from E.O. 12,333, as interpreted, applied, overseen by agency Offices of General Counsel and Offices of Inspector General, with violations reported to the Intelligence Oversight Board of the President's Foreign Intelligence Advisory Board.

Before any technology that might be developed by IARPA could be used in an operational setting, the use of the analytic tool would need to be examined pursuant to E.O. 12,333 and other applicable law to determine how the tool could be used consistent with the agency's U.S. person guidelines. As discussed above, these guidelines are extensive. For example, the Department of Defense (DOD) guidelines, which are unclassified, consist of sixty-four pages of detailed procedures and rules governing the intelligence activities of DOD components that affect U.S. persons.

In addition, because IARPA anticipates that capabilities derived from some of its research efforts could potentially have some impact on privacy or civil liberties, it has undertaken a separate, but related, research effort into privacy protecting technologies, described in detail above.

Tailored policy, privacy and civil liberties guidance has also been developed to address specific problems posed by particular IARPA projects in coordination with ODNI's Privacy and Civil Liberties Office. For example, KDD has developed policy guidance, which is awaiting review and approval, to govern its planned joint activities with law enforcement and the Department of Homeland Security.

Likewise, the Tangram project has implemented specific restrictions on the data sources to which its researchers have access, in response to guidance from CLPO.

IARPA will continue its close working relationship with the ODNI Civil Liberties and Privacy Office to develop additional policy, privacy and civil liberties guidance as needed. The Civil Liberties and Privacy Office is headed by the Civil Liberties Protection Officer, a position established by the Intelligence Reform and Terrorism Prevention Act of 2004 (IRTPA), and reports directly to the DNI.

The goal of the CLPO is to help the intelligence community accomplish its national security mission in a way that remains true to the Constitution and protects privacy and civil liberties. Under the IRTPA, the CLPO's duties include ensuring that the protection of civil liberties and privacy is appropriately incorporated in the policies of the ODNI and the intelligence community, overseeing compliance by the ODNI with legal requirements relating to civil liberties and privacy, reviewing complaints about potential abuses of privacy and civil liberties in ODNI programs and activities.

Perhaps most relevant to IARPA, the CLPO is also charged with ensuring that technologies sustain, and do not erode, privacy. As the intelligence community seeks to use new tools, techniques, and approaches to keep the country safe, so too the ODNI must develop and use new tools, techniques, and approaches to protect civil liberties and privacy.

The CLPO works through the intelligence community's civil liberties protection infrastructure -- and recommends improvements where needed -- to ensure that privacy and civil liberties issues are identified and addressed as early as feasible, and that safeguards are formulated and implemented to protect privacy and civil liberties. The CLPO enhances, and does not replace, the civil liberties protection functions of existing offices and mechanisms, and seeks to ensure that new protective functions and mechanisms -- such as civil liberties positions as they are created in other agencies, and the Privacy and Civil Liberties Oversight Board -- interact effectively with the intelligence community to further strengthen privacy and civil liberties safeguards.

REFERENCES

[1] IARPA invests in cutting-edge research projects that have the potential to result in revolutionary, game-changing capabilities for the IC. Should such advanced research projects prove feasible, they may subsequently be transitioned into settings involving operational use.

[2] RDEC is a testing environment that contains the data sources used by these and other projects, and is described in more detail below in response to the Data Mining Reporting Act's question regarding data sources.

[3] A unique research effort within the intelligence community.

INDEX

D

E

F

G

H

I

J

N

O

P

Q

R

S

T

U

V

W